D0072843

VIRGINIA WOOLF'S
REDISCOVERED ESSAYS

GARLAND REFERENCE LIBRARY
OF THE HUMANITIES
(VOL. 686)

VIRGINIA WOOLF'S REDISCOVERED ESSAYS
Sources and Allusions

Elizabeth Steele

GARLAND PUBLISHING, INC. • NEW YORK & LONDON
1987

Library of Congress Cataloging-in-Publication Data

Steele, Elizabeth.
  Virginia Woolf's rediscovered essays.

  (Garland reference library of the humanities ;
vol. 686)
  Includes index.
  1. Woolf, Virginia, 1882–1941—Bibliography.
2. Woolf, Virginia, 1882–1941—Sources.   3. Woolf,
Virginia, 1882–1941—Knowledge—Literature.   I. Title.
II. Series: Garland reference library of the
humanities ; v. 686.
Z8984.2.S743   1987   016.824'912   86-25725
[PR6045.072]
ISBN 0-8240-8527-2

Printed on acid-free, 250-year-life paper
Manufactured in the United States of America

TO MY BELOVED HUSBAND

CONTENTS

PREFACE

As its title suggests, *Virginia Woolf's Rediscovered Essays: Sources and Allusions* is intended as a survey of sources for, and literary allusions within, a vital body of literature heretofore unexplored in book form. Many cultured persons, including scholars, are unaware that Virginia Woolf, though known the world over for her exciting lyrical novels and six impressive books of collected essays,[1] wrote as many essays again, which until recently remained buried in periodical files on both sides of the Atlantic. The main role of the present study, as I see it, is to act as an introduction to these rediscovered works.

In *Virginia Woolf and Her World* John Lehmann[2] describes the mass of essays and reviews written by this famous 20th-century author as a corpus "perfectly compounded of imagination and wit, ... always a delight in its freshness, its sureness of touch, its measured but easy flow; her lucid intelligence plays over everything." Mr. Lehmann adds, "Her power of visualization, and her skill in getting to the heart of a subject, are exemplified again and again....

"Nor does she confine her sympathy to the great figures; she has an extraordinary capacity for making an odd

character live...." One might go on indefinitely quoting
Mr. Lehmann's praise of "this miraculous body of critical
work," were there not the danger--entirely unfounded--of
making him appear her sole appreciator. To dispel that
illusion, another quotation, this time from American
critic Stanley Hyman, who evaluates Woolf's essays as
"making literary figures, schools, and periods come
alive.... She summons up their atmosphere, their quality
of life, their very aroma." He calls them "invaluable."[3]

Regrettably, however, the earliest essays, written
when she was Virginia Stephen and many of which are hard
to find, have not been available to scholars and general
readers up to this time.

From 1904 to 1941, Virginia Woolf wrote more than
five hundred essays, some two hundred and seventy of
which are at the moment out of print. For example, of
the 246 essays published by her favored periodical, the
London *Times Literary Supplement*, and listed in the last
edition of B.J. Kirkpatrick's *Bibliography of Virginia
Woolf*,[4] only 93 have until now been collected and easily
available.

Thus, as Mark Goldman points out,[5] even "sympathetic"
readers have been unable to "approach the large number of
Mrs. Woolf's ... uncollected essays with anything resem-
bling" a thorough reading. True, "most of ... [them]
were originally reviews"; but many were "deliberately
conceived critical essays...." The conclusions of "com-
mentators whose evidence has been," whether forcibly or

voluntarily, "limited to certain essays" will continue to be incomplete until the rest of her works in this genre are available for consultation.

Observation shows that although her collected essays are read and appreciated by more and more scholars and the public at large each year, the bulk of Woolf's uncollected essays has remained unknown. "The materials, ... scattered in a great variety of places" [see Appendix A, *infra*], have been "hard to get at."[6] Fortunately, however, with the publication of the complete essays in six volumes, edited by Andrew McNeillie and soon to be issued in London and New York,[7] the situation is about to change.

While most of the rediscovered essays are less complex than the "collected" ones, some are as elaborate as anything composed by Virginia Woolf in this genre. "[T]o read her earliest work chronologically," Edward Hungerford reminds us,[8] "and ... note the gradual signs of increasing power and certainty in method and idea" is clearly important to those who would speak with authority about Virginia Woolf as a creative thinker.

"Unless one considers ... her reviews and articles" *in toto*, adds Suzanne Henig,[9] "(not just the *Common Readers* ... or the many posthumous collections," which have given an incomplete picture), Woolf's "critical method [cannot] become apparent."

Published in Autumn 1983, *Virginia Woolf's Literary Sources and Allusions: A Guide to the Essays*[10] dealt with the 250 critical essays written by Virginia Woolf and

collected in book form up to that point. The present volume, a sequel, deals with the 270 critical essays printed
in magazines and newspapers over the years but heretofore
uncollected. Since both segments, the "collected" and
the "uncollected," will be joined in the six-volume complete essays, this study has an advantage over the previous one of dealing with the relatively "new" pieces--an
opportunity for the casual reader or the scholar to become
acquainted, in organized fashion, with material s/he probably has not seen before.

Besides the charts of sources and allusions, modeled
on those in the 1983 volume, this book contains an introduction intended to acquaint the reader with the history
and breadth-of-content of these heretofore almost unknown
essays (the majority of which Woolf composed before becom-
ing a novelist). A list of books formerly belonging to
the Woolfs and newly purchased from some of their heirs--a
list germane to both this and the previous study of Sources
and Allusions--is included as an Appendix.

Notes for the Preface

1. Here I refer to the four volumes of *Collected
Essays* (London: Hogarth; New York: Harcourt, Brace and
World, 1966-67), edited by Leonard Woolf; *Contemporary
Writers* (London: Hogarth, 1965; New York: Harcourt, Brace
and World, 1966), edited by Jean Guiguet; and *Books and
Portraits* (London: Hogarth, 1977; New York: Harcourt Brace
Jovanovich, 1978), edited by Mary Lyon.

2. London: Thames and Hudson, 1975. P. 100.

3. *The Armed Vision*. (1948). Rev. ed., abr. New York: Vintage Books, 1955. P. 107.

4. (1957). 3rd ed. Oxford: Clarendon, 1980.

5. Morris I. [*sic*] Goldman, *Virginia Woolf and the Art of Criticism*. (U. of Minnesota, 1959). Ann Arbor, Mich.: University Microfilms, 1975. Pp. 4-6. Mr. Goldman's work has also appeared in book form: Mark Goldman, *The Reader's Art: Virginia Woolf as Literary Critic*. The Hague: Mouton, 1976.

6. Suzanne Henig, *The Literary Criticism of Virginia Woolf*. (New York U., 1968). Ann Arbor, Mich.: University Microfilms, 1969. P. viii.

7. *The Essays of Virginia Woolf*, edited by Andrew McNeillie. Volume I is expected in 1987.

8. Edward A. Hungerford, *The Narrow Bridge of Art: Virginia Woolf's Early Criticism, 1905-1925*. (New York U., 1960). Ann Arbor, Mich.: University Microfilms, 1960. P. 22.

9. Henig, p. 256.

10. Elizabeth Steele, *Virginia Woolf's Literary Sources and Allusions*. New York: Garland, 1983.

ACKNOWLEDGMENTS

It is hard to know whom to thank first. If I could, I would make two parallel columns. On the left I would put three names representing those unsung heroes of the academic world--the writers of unpublished Ph.D. dissertations; in this case: Robert Ferebee, Suzanne Henig and Edward Hungerford. All have written on Virginia Woolf as essayist. (For titles, see notes to the Preface and Chapter 1.) Ed Hungerford particularly has been a helpful friend and colleague down the years. The dissertations of all three have served to remind me of the kinds of background facts the public needs to know to better appreciate Virginia Woolf's rediscovered essays.

My right-hand column would open with the names of Jo-anne Hartough, enterprising director of the Interlibrary Loan service at the University of Toledo's William S. Carlson Library, and her staff; continue with Leila Luedeking, indispensable curator of the Woolf Collection, Washington State University Library; and close with Andrew McNeillie, editor of the forthcoming multivolume complete essays by Virginia Woolf whose friendly cooperation has smoothed the pathway these past several months. To him and to Quentin Bell and Angelica Garnett (literary executors, Estate of Virginia Woolf) I owe the ability to quote the contents of Chapter 3.

Warm thanks must also go to Dr. John Guido, head of the Manuscripts, Archives and Special Collections department at Washington State, for permission to transmit materials in Appendix B.

INTRODUCTION

Chapter 1

THE REDISCOVERED ESSAYS

1904-41

Louis Kronenberg in an essay on "Virginia Woolf as Critic" remarks, " ... Mrs. Woolf forged her criticism into something quite as distinctive as her novels, and the best of it may well survive everything else she wrote except *To the Lighthouse* and *Mrs. Dalloway*, and may conceivably survive them."[1]

In critic Mark Goldman's opinion, what she says of Madame de Sévigné's personality may be applied also to her own: "She was a born critic, and a critic whose judgments were inborn, unhesitating. She is always referring her impressions to a standard--hence the incisiveness, the depth, and the comedy that make [her] spontaneous statements so illuminating."[2]

Though nearly always good-humored, Woolf is also tenacious. Her stance is that of a contender, lightly poised, polite, but eager for the fray and alert to take advantage. "Iron hand in velvet glove" would be putting it too strongly. Closer would be Robert Frost's image of the "silken tent" (in his poem of that name) which, attached to its site by strong ropes, blows freely, fearlessly in the wind.

One reason we enjoy reading Virginia Woolf's essays is that she so clearly enjoyed creating them. In 1921 she notes in her diary, "Whatever book I read bubbles up in my mind as part of an article I want to write."[3] As late as 1939 she commented, "Ideas for articles obsess me." She called herself "ravaged by" them.[4]

Although Virginia Woolf scholars who have a strong interest in her essays do not always realize that less than fifty percent of them have been collected to date, yet this kind of writing spanned her creative career from her first article, submitted shortly after her father, Leslie Stephen, died in 1904, until shortly before her own death in 1941.

Since the publication of B.J. Kirkpatrick's *Bibliography of Virginia Woolf*, 3rd edition,[5] in 1980, it has become possible to pinpoint the start of her career. She started professional book reviewing at the age of twenty-two, when her first essay appeared in the *Guardian* (London) on December 14, 1904.

Before settling down to an analysis, a quick overview follows of those who published her essays for the next four decades: On March 10, 1905, Virginia Stephen began a thirty-two-year association with the *Times Literary Supplement* (or *TLS*). The *National Review*, the *Speaker*, and *Cornhill* magazine accepted some early pieces; but the *TLS* published most of her articles until 1919, when she commenced to write for the newly refurbished *Athenaeum*. The *New Statesman* began printing Woolf's essays in 1920; in 1923 she started submitting to American periodicals which came to include the *New Republic*, the *Literary Review* of the *New York Evening Post*, and *Vogue* (both New York and London), among others. Back in England, the *Athenaeum* had become the *Nation and Athenaeum* in 1924. Her husband, Leonard, was its literary editor, and Woolf wrote for this journal regularly. Soon many of her essays were being placed concurrently in periodicals in Britain and the United States. By 1929, she had published sporadically in various journals such as the *Bookman* (New York), *T.P.'s Weekly*, and *Forum* (New York); still, most of her pieces appeared in the *TLS*, the *Nation and Athenaeum*, the *New Republic*, and the *New York Herald Tribune Books*.

Nation and Athenaeum became the *New Statesman and Nation* in 1931, with Leonard no longer literary editor, but Virginia continued writing for them now and then. The *Yale Review*, *Good Housekeeping* (London), and the *Atlantic Monthly* accepted some of her later pieces. She ceased to write for the *TLS* in 1937. Three weeks before her death, Virginia Woolf's final essay appeared in the *New Statesman and Nation*.

To trace chronologically, article by article, Woolf's rediscovered essays requires more space than need be given here. In summary, most of the 275 articles currently not in print, though soon to be, are early ones (1904-15) from the *Guardian*, the *TLS*, and the *Cornhill*; or middle ones (1916-32) from the *TLS*, the *New Republic*, and the *Nation and Athenaeum*. All but two of the twenty-nine critical essays written from 1933 to 1941 are now in print (one of the former is in obituary form).

The Guardian (thirty-two items, only two collected, one of which is a personal essay), while "fine as a beginning," as Suzanne Henig says,6 "was published by the Anglican church"; whereas Virginia "had been brought up in a household where her father, an ordained Anglican priest, had left the church as an acknowledged agnostic," and her mother, Julia Stephen, had written a long article (unpublished) on behalf of "Agnostic Women."7

The last piece Virginia authored for *The Guardian*
appeared on   February 13, 1907, except for an obituary of
her Quaker aunt, Caroline Stephen, published there April
21, 1909.   Meanwhile, "through the good offices of a
friend" (Kitty Maxse, the original of "Mrs. Dalloway"),[8]
some of her manuscripts "found their way into the hands of
Bruce Richmond," editor of the "respected and powerful"
TLS, and "she later met [him] at a tea party."[9]   As her
diary reports, he "very soon came to business.... [and]
asked if 'we' The Times, that is, might send me books for
review ... --So I said yes--and thus my work gets estab-
lished, and I suppose, I shall soon have as much as I can
do--which is certainly satisfactory."[10] (As in the *Guardian*,
her articles appeared anonymously.)

     B.J. Kirkpatrick's *Bibliography* shows the *TLS* con-
tributions beginning in 1905, March 10, and as Robert Ferebee puts it, "the educated, literate readers of this journal became her most consistent audience"[11] till she ceased
writing for it in 1937.

     Ten reviews (none yet collected) account for the out-
put of 1907.   In 1906, the year of her favorite brother,
Thoby's, death, Virginia had begun work on her first novel,
"an act which was not to terminate in publication"[12] till
almost ten years later.   She wrote twenty essays between
January and August that year, all still uncollected.   Thoby Stephen died in late autumn.

     Three years after a series of debacles had begun--
personal illness (brought on by her father's demise in
1904), the loss of Thoby by death and her sister Vanessa
by marriage--Virginia Stephen returned with vigor to reviewing and her output included twenty articles (ten uncollected) in 1908; sixteen (eight uncollected) in 1909.

     Her early *TLS* essays were, usually, a few paragraphs
and, by Robert Ferebee's calculation, up to 1,200 words
long.   The uncollected "A Swan and Her Friends," for example, "took up three-quarters of a column and appeared
on a back page.   Later, as Virginia Woolf gained stature
and scope,"[13] her essays consisted of as many as 4,000
words.   They often appeared on the front page of the
Supplement, occupying several columns.   The fact that this
happened as early as 1909, Edward Hungerford believes,
shows her entrance into "a higher class of book reviewers--
a more experienced class," at least.[14]

     The previous year she had written six articles for
the prestigious *Cornhill* magazine.   These reviews (three
uncollected) concerned "persons who had been in the public
eye: the most famous actress of the nineteenth century
[Sarah Bernhardt], an American president [Theodore Roose-
velt], a distinguished newspaper editor [John Delane of
the *Times*], the mistress of a king [i.e., Louis XIV], and

two British women of the nobility [Lady Dorothy Nevill
and Lady Elizabeth Holland]." Only four reviews, all collected, date from 1910. Why Virginia published so little
that year is partly explained by an editors' note in Volume I of her *Letters*:   "In the early part of the year,
weakened perhaps by overwork ... , she seemed ... to be
on the verge of insanity, and successive visits to Corn-
wall, Dorset and a rented house near Canterbury failed to
restore her. In late June she re-entered the mental
nursing-home at Twickenham for six weeks, but her condi-
tion was not serious enough to prevent her from writing
letters, and in them she ridiculed her situation more
than she craved sympathy."[15] There was also the fact
that her Quaker aunt, Caroline Stephen--whom the "children" called "Nun"--had died the previous year and left
Virginia, alone of all the siblings, 2,500 pounds (the
others received one hundred each). Perhaps the pressure
to earn seemed temporarily less than it had before.

The essays in 1910, 1911, and 1912, all written for
the *TLS*, depended on biographical treatment of their subjects. "Eight articles [four of them uncollected] in
three years: not a very large production," comments Edward Hungerford,[16] compared with later, busier years like
1917 (thirty-five reviews, twenty-three uncollected) or
1918 (forty-three, twenty-one uncollected).

1913 concluded the first period of Woolf's work as a
reviewer: only three articles (all uncollected) are listed
for that year in Kirkpatrick's *Bibliography*; none for
1914 or 1915. An extended illness after her marriage ac-
counts for this notable gap. She was able to do whatever
editorial work was needed to complete *The Voyage Out*
(published, 1915, in an edition of 2,000 copies), but she
did no reviewing for at least two years. From a letter
which Virginia wrote to Lytton Strachey on October 22,
1915, however, we find that her convalescence was over at
last. "I should think I had read 600 books since we met,"
she brags.[17]

Thus, as Edward Hungerford expresses it, "a more experienced ... Virginia Woolf began another period in her
career." Returning in January 1916 to reviewing exclu-
sively for the *TLS*, rested and refreshed, "she now spoke
as a published novelist."[18] Looking back, she had also,
during the years 1904 through 1913, written over a hundred articles of varying lengths on a variety of topics,
usually literary. Among the (heretofore uncollected)
products of her pen, preceding publication of *The Voyage
Out*, are reviews discussing Wordsworth family letters,
the Carlyles--Jane and Thomas--, Christina Rossetti, the
Duke and Duchess of Newcastle-upon-Tyne, George Gissing,
and many others.

In 1916 she produced fifteen articles, including reviews (eight still uncollected), and in 1917 and 1918, as
mentioned, thirty-five and forty-three, respectively. An
amazing record, considering that these years covered the
climax of World War I, during which "everyone near to her
was either a conscientious objector or declared medically
unfit to serve," Suzanne Henig reminds us.[19]

Early in 1919, having finished her second novel,
Night and Day, and released from tnat discipline and the
moral strain of war, she looked around for new markets to
conquer. As Edward Hungerford recounts it, "[J]ust at
this time a fresh viewpoint on life and letters was being
introduced in London by the publication of the reorganized
periodical the *Athenaeum*, under the editorship of John
Middleton Murry. Murry, through Katherine Mansfield, had
asked Virginia Woolf to become a contributor in February,
1919, and her first article appeared on April 25...."[20]

Altogether she wrote seventeen lively articles for
Murry and Mansfield during a two-year period--eleven, including two personal essays, in 1919 (four uncollected)
and six (three uncollected) in 1920. Her fellow-contribu-
tors included T.S. Eliot, Lytton Strachey, Leonard Woolf,
Katherine Mansfield, and E.M. Forster, and a glance at
Virginia's contributions reveals "a lighter,... more auda-
cious ...tone," seldom displayed in the *TLS*.[21]

During 1920 she produced a total of forty-four (seventeen uncollected) articles and reviews, including
thirty-three for the faithful Richmond. After 1921 she
reviewed books less frequently than before. For the *TLS*
after that year, her maximum was four articles in any
twelve-month period. To Edward Hungerford, the reasons
for this seem obvious: "(1) she undoubtedly was better
paid by other periodicals, especially the American ...
ones; and (2) ... although retaining her respect and ad-
miration for Bruce Richmond," she found the *TLS* atmosphere
"stuffy,"[22] especially after the *Athenaeum*.

For a period of five months in 1921 (July-November)
she ceased writing essays in order to complete her
precedent-breaking novel *Jacob's Room*, published in 1922.
Otherwise her articles continued at a good pace: twelve
(seven uncollected); and, though nothing was published between January 12 and July 15, 1922, the rest of that year
brought five pieces to the fore.

During 1923 she added two other important periodicals
to the list which gladly accepted her work--the *Nation and
Athenaeum* and the *New Republic*. Sometimes the American
journal reprinted, word-for-word, from the *Nation and
Athenaeum*, but not often; and she continued to publish in
both regularly for years. In the *Nation and Athenaeum*
over a hundred articles, long and short, of which three-

fourths remain uncollected, appeared up to the end of
1930 (when the periodical was absorbed into the *New
Statesman and Nation*).[23]

The last decade in Virginia Woolf's life saw a de-
cline in her critical output. Fewer than forty literary
articles were published during those years. One agrees
with Suzanne Henig that the decrease may be "attributed
to a number of factors: declining financial problems (ac-
cording to Leonard Woolf) ... , the deaths in the thirties
of a number of intimate friends" including fellow-critic
and literary historian Lytton Strachey, "the end of her
reviewing career with *The Times*, [and] the onset of the
second World War...."[24]

No critical articles, only an obituary of literary
hostess Ottoline Morrell, appeared in 1938; four essays
were printed in 1939 and eight more in 1940--one of which,
"Georgiana and Florence" (about two ancestors of her
friend the poet Edith Sitwell), remains uncollected. In
1941, she published only two articles before her death.

Concerning the essays, her obituary might well read:
"Virginia Woolf was a great essayist, perhaps the greatest
essayist of the twentieth century. She is certainly the
first woman essayist of her stature.... A different part
of her mind created the essays than that which wrote the
novels or the diaries or the pamphlets, but, after all,
the same woman, the same perfectionist, the same genius
wrote essays almost daily for the greater part of her
adult life."[25]

Variety of Topics

As we have seen, Virginia Woolf was at work regularly
from 1904 to 1941, estimating a new writer or a classic
one, recording her impressions about novels, memoirs, biographies, literary criticism, history, essays, letters,
diaries, travel narratives, etc. She also took on poetry and drama. To quote Edward Hungerford, "Everything
that can be imagined of a literary nature ... came her
way"[1]--with fiction represented more than any other genre.

John Lehmann[2] divides these essays into categories:
"[a] portraits and [b] assessments of individual writers,"
male and female, past and present, from various nations;
[c] a solid body of polemical articles that were "important in relation to her own ideals or aims in writing";
and [d] the "'lives of the obscure.'"

Of the essays which are still uncollected, Robert
Ferebee[3] estimates that about sixty-five percent are on

literary topics, thirty percent are biographical and five
percent are "reflective" (personal).

Literary Topics: Some Notes

    Americana. Though Woolf herself never came to
America, her ties with it began before her birth. Her
father, Sir Leslie Stephen, himself an outstanding lit-
erary critic, had travelled in America and numbered among
his friends the luminaries of New England *belles lettres*.
Massachusetts poet James Russell Lowell, Ambassador to
Great Britain when Virginia was born, was her godfather.
Among American authors reviewed in her rediscovered essays
are Edith Wharton (*The House of Mirth*); Edgar Lee Masters
(*The Great Valley*); William Dean Howells (*The Son of Royal
Langbrith*), and a study of Henry James--whom she knew well
personally--by Joseph Warren Beach. Possibly Woolf's major (uncollected) effort in the field of Americana appeared
on pages 21, 144-45 of *Hearst's International Combined
with Cosmopolitan* (New York), April 1938 issue: "America
Which I Have Never Seen Interests Me Most in This Cosmopolitan World of Today"--a personal essay.

    Women. At an early stage in her career, when con-
fronted with the task of reviewing a book about Catherine
de Medici, Virginia Woolf failed in the assignment. Her
1905 diary tells the story:⁴

    March 10: "A letter from Richmond to offer me Miss
[Edith] Sichels Catherine de Medici to review column and
a half--I told him I was not [at] home in Mediaeval Per-
iod--which is strictly true!"

    Her main problem was one of verification; March 12:
"I read a good bit of Sichel, & tried to find out something about France or the Reformation from other histories.
I find that she is not too learned: I shall be able to
[do] criticism on general grounds, & already some things
occur to me to say. She is a clever woman, hunting for a
style--but I cant correct her facts--"

    March 16: "Started my Sichel review for the Times,
but it was heavy going. It is a satirical fact that when
I am allowed ½ a column I can always fill two and when I
am to have as much space as I like, I cant screw out words
at any price.... At every step I tremble guiltily, I withdraw, to temper my expressions. So it will be dull."

    April 25: "A letter ... from Bruce Richmond, with
the unfortunate Sichel review which has been hanging like
a stone round my neck, and haunting my nights. It is not
'academic' enough--sorry he misled me--an excellent article, but a professed historian is needed to which I cor-
dially agree, and Sichel goes to the waste paper basket!"

But she made up for her hesitancy later and often, by
undertaking to review many books by and about women as ar-
cane sometimes, even, as Catherine de Medici. In fact,
they became one of her favorite subjects. As Edward Hungerford puts it,[5] "The thread of [this] preoccupation winds
itself throughout" her rediscovered criticism.

    British Male Writers. But the journals were as eager
for her reviews of male works as for her essays on women.
To quote Suzanne Henig,[6] "Virginia Woolf's critical ideas
manifested themselves in ... specific observations" concerning writers of both sexes: Shakespeare was the greatest British author--if not in the world; she admired Conrad and approved of Gissing, Austen and the Brontës. She
disapproved of Arnold Bennett and Edmund Gosse, and indeed
most of the Victorians. The greatest modern fictionists
were Russians. Fewer of her uncollected articles are on
male literary figures than on women authors, and include
only one cluster on a male writer of the first rank--five
essays on Joseph Conrad. Other pieces dealt with Samuel
Butler, Sir Walter Scott, Charles Dickens and George Meredith. Among minor British male novelists who contributed
books for assessment down the years she was reviewing were
W.E. Norris (surprisingly a favorite of Woolf's), William
DeMorgan, Oliver Onions and Anthony Hope.

    Poetry. From her earliest reviews, Virginia Woolf
explored, intermittently, the work of poets. A personal
friendship grew up between the Woolfs and T.S. Eliot, beginning in 1919. She took great interest in his work (the
Woolfs' Hogarth Press first published *The Waste Land*, in
1922), but most of her poetry reviews concerned themselves
chiefly with more minor writers. Her respect for nature,
however, drew her to the great Romantic poets, especially
Wordsworth. Poetry, as a whole, attracted her and the
number of her uncollected reviews in this genre is sub-
stantial.

    Drama. Seventeen, in all, of Woolf's rediscovered
articles deal with the dramatists and their work. Five
theater pieces are biographical: "Rachel," "A Player Under
Three Reigns" (Forbes Robertson), "On Some of the Old Actors" (Augustine Daly), "Guests and Memories" (Henry Taylor)
and "On the Stage" (George Arliss). She also wrote reviews
of some live performances. Those listed in Kirkpatrick and
still uncollected include: *The Higher Court*, by M.E.M.
Young, "performed at a Sunday subscription theatre," April
1920; *The Cherry Orchard*, by Anton Chekhov, performed in
the Arts Theatre, July 1920; Congreve's *Love for Love* (a
play she had always admired), performed at the Lyric Theatre, Hammersmith, April 1921; and a joint performance of
The Tale of a Soldier (Stravinsky) and *A Lover's Complaint*
(Shakespeare) at the A.D.C. Theatre, November 1928. The
most interesting of these is probably her assessment of
The Cherry Orchard.

Russian Literature. It was in 1917, coincidentally the year of the Russian Revolution, that Virginia Woolf began a series of *estimes* of Tolstoy, Dostoevsky, Chekhov and other classic Russian authors, usually as translated by her friend Constance Garnett. One rediscovered piece is biographical, based on a Hogarth Press publication, *Reminiscences of Leo Nicolayevitch Tolstoi*, by Maxim Gorky, reviewed (unsigned) in the *New Statesman*, August 7, 1920.

Literary Criticism. A number of the uncollected reviews discuss literary critics, from Arthur Symons to William Dean Howells, W.E. Henley to Augustine Birrell, Sir Walter Raleigh to Viscount Harberton. It is exhilarating to follow an agile mind like Woolf's as it skates across the ice of literary theory, her own or others', making arabesques along the way. Such essays, Edward Hungerford points out,[7] "cast a well-defined light upon her own [critical] beliefs," since in writing about critics she had to judge their methods. While some were Woolf's contemporaries, "her most penetrating comments are reserved for older writers" like Edmund Gosse and Coventry Patmore.

Biography

Virginia Woolf's biographical vignettes are as valuable as her literary criticism. Where the writer's life and works can scarcely be separated, she shows the latter developing out of the former. Where the portrait of a person furnishes Woolf's entire subject matter, we observe, as Edward Hungerford says,[8] her "impressionistic method at work," selecting details to fit an overall theme. He gives as examples "goodness" of character in the case of Frances Willard, "bird-brained flightiness" in the case of Lady Dorothy Nevill.

For classification purposes, however, it is necessary to separate miniature "portraits" like the above from essays which discuss the art of writing biography (e.g., "A Character Sketch" [August 13, 1920]), thus filling another function altogether.

In the former she uses her sources (a biography or memoirs, letters, diaries, etc.) to recreate a specific era. Their contents become windows for looking into others' lives.

The purpose of portraits like "The Duke and Duchess of Newcastle-upon-Tyne," for instance, was not only to review a new biography [see chart] about the famous pair but to recreate their personalities as vividly as possible in the space of two newspaper columns (here, those of the *TLS*). "[S]uch articles ... [are] permanently interesting,"

comments Edward Hungerford,[9] "transcending the reviewer's
task and taking their place in the realm of [creative]
literary essays."

   At a distance from these portraits are the various
articles, written by Woolf, discussing biography as a
genre. And somewhere between these two categories are
essays in which the functions are mixed (e.g., "Scott's
Character" [1921], half portrait, half critical essay).

   Despite frequent anomalous subjects like socialist
Ernest Belfort Bax, eccentric Margot Asquith, or American
president "Teddy" Roosevelt, more than anything else Virginia Woolf wrote, in her essays, about the literary life:
the lives of authors and their works. As an author herself and the daughter and niece of authors, this was what
she understood most thoroughly. Jean Guiguet, in *Virginia
Woolf and Her Works*,[10] speaks of Woolf in her essays,
especially the biographical ones, appealing to her
sources, "these writers of diaries or letters, these
friends, patrons, relatives of famous authors, like so
many stage supers or members of the chorus." This bears
out Stanley Hyman's general assessment of the essays as
"closet drama."[11]

   The following list (pp. 13ff.) disperses the biographical pieces among various headings. Those on well
known writers--with two exceptions, Tolstoy and Byron--
are generally found under the genre they specialized in,
or under "Major Women Writers." Some fifty percent of
Woolf's biographical essays are written about famous people. The remaining ones concern the lives of lesser-
known, even "obscure," inhabitants of history and the
arts. Woolf's essays on less famous women--about one-
third of the biographical pieces--have their own category:
"Women (General)."

Familiar Essays

   As used by Robert Ferebee,[12] "reflective" is the term
which covers a miscellaneous group of Woolf's articles
more commonly called, as they are here, "familiar" essays
(though both terms have limitations). Their subjects include street music, traveling ("An Andalusian Inn"), walk-
ing ("Heard on the Downs"), landmarks and laughter. Scattered throughout her career, published in journals as var-
ied as the *National Review*, *Guardian*, *Athenaeum*, *Woman's
Leader*, and the *Times*, they have much in common with her
short stories, especially the early ones.

In the following list, essays under each heading are ar-
ranged by date, so special emphases may be traced in a
historical framework.

Americana
(rediscovered essays)

Dec. 14, 1904	Review of *The Son of Royal Langbrith* (Howells)
Feb. 8, 1905	"A Belle of the Fifties"
Feb. 22, 1905	"Mr. Henry James's Latest Novel"
May 31, 1905	"The American Woman"
Nov. 15, 1905	Review of *The House of Mirth* (Wharton)
Nov. 17, 1905	Review of *The Debtor* (Wilkins)
July 13, 1906	Review of *Coniston* (Churchill)
August 1908	"The Book on the Table: *A Week at the White House*"(Hale)
Apr. 12, 1917	"A Talker [Edgar Lee Masters]"
Dec. 26, 1918	"The Method of Henry James"
Apr. 3, 1919	"Washington Irving"
Jan. 29, 1920	"An American Poet [Vachel Lindsay]"
April 1938	"America, Which I Have Never Seen ..." --no chart

Women (General)
(rediscovered essays)

Jan. 25, 1905	"The Feminine Note in Fiction"
Aug. 26, 1905	"Their Passing Hour"
Jan. 13, 1906	"The Sister of Frederic the Great"
July 11, 1906	"The Bluest of the Blue"
July 28, 1906	"Sweetness--Long Drawn Out"
July 26, 1907	"Lady Fanshawe's Memoirs"
Nov. 7, 1907	Review of *The Last Days of Marie Antoin-ette* (Lenôtre, ed.)
Nov. 14, 1907	Review of *A Swan and Her Friends* (Lucas)
April 1908	"The Book on the Table: *The Memoirs of Lady Dorothy Nevill*"
Sept. 3, 1908	"Scottish Women"
October 1908	"The Book on the Table: *Louise de la Vallière*" (Lair)
Oct. 29, 1908	"Chateau and Country Life"
Nov. 19, 1908	"*Blackstick Papers*"
Apr. 21, 1909	"In Memoriam: Caroline Emelia Stephen"
Nov. 25, 1909	"A Cookery Book"
Nov. 28, 1912	"Frances Willard"
Dec. 6, 1917	"Mr. Gladstone's Daughter"
March 6, 1919	"Lady Ritchie"
Nov. 17, 1923	"The Chinese Shoe"
Feb. 23, 1924	Review of *Letters and Journals of Anne Chalmers*
June 7, 1924	Review of *Marie Elizabeth Towneley: A Memoir*
Oct. 2, 1924	"The Schoolroom Floor"

Nov. 8, 1924	Review of *Memories of a Militant* (Kenney)
Nov. 22, 1924	"These Were Muses"
Jan. 30, 1925	Review of *Mary Elizabeth Haldane: A Record of a Hundred Years*
May 16, 1925	"Gipsy or Governess?"
Aug. 1, 1925	"'Pattledom'"
Feb. 6, 1926	Review of *Queen Alexandra the Well-Beloved* (Villiers)
March 20, 1926	Review of *Reminiscences of Mrs. Comyns Carr* (Adam, ed.)
March 20, 1926	Review of *The Flurried Years* (V. Hunt)
May 26, 1928	Review of *The Book of Catherine Wells*
Sept. 29, 1928	Review of *The Diaries of Mary, Countess of Meath*
December 1932	"Portrait of a Londoner"--no chart
July 22, 1937	"Obituary--Miss Janet Case"--no chart
Apr. 28, 1938	"Lady Ottoline Morrell"
March 31, 1940	"Georgiana and Florence"

Major Women Writers

(rediscovered essays)

Aug. 2, 1905	"The Letters of Jane Welsh Carlyle"
Nov. 12, 1908	"Letters of Christina Rossetti"
Apr. 1, 1909	"More Carlyle Letters"
May 8, 1913	"Jane Austen"
Apr. 13, 1916	"Charlotte Brontë"
Dec. 13, 1917	"Charlotte Brontë"
May 6, 1920	"An Imperfect Lady [Mary Russell Mitford]"
May 26, 1920	"A Good Daughter [Mitford]"
May 28, 1920	"The Wrong Way of Reading [Mitford]"
March 9, 1921	"Great Names: George Eliot"
Dec. 15, 1923	"Jane Austen at Sixty"
Apr. 18, 1925	Review of *The Letters of Mary Russell Mitford*
Oct. 30, 1926	"George Eliot"

Novels by Women

(rediscovered essays)

March 22, 1905	Review of *By Beach and Bogland* (Fisher)
May 10, 1905	Review of *Nancy Stair* (Lane)
May 24, 1905	Review of *A Dark Lantern* (Robins)
July 19, 1905	Review of *Rose of Lone Farm* (Hayden)
Nov. 17, 1905	Review of *The Making of Michael* (Reynolds)
Nov. 17, 1905	Review of *A Flood Tide* (Debenham)
Dec. 6, 1905	Review of *The Brown House and Cordelia* (Booth)
Dec. 15, 1905	"Two Irish Novels"
Dec. 20, 1905	Review of *The Tower of Siloam* (Graham)
Jan. 10, 1906	Review of *After His Kind* (Henderson)
Jan. 23, 1906	Review of *Blanche Esmead* (Maitland)
Feb. 16, 1906	Review of *A Supreme Moment* (Mrs. H. Synge)

Feb. 16, 1906   Review of *The Scholar's Daughter* (Harraden)
June 15, 1906   Review of *The Compromise* (Gerard)
May 10, 1907   Review of *Fraulein Schmidt and Mr. Anstruther* ("Elizabeth")
May 24, 1907   Review of *The Glen o'Weeping* (M. Bowen)
Apr. 25, 1918   "Second Marriage [Alice Meynell]"
Oct. 9, 1919   "*Madeleine* [Hope Mirrlees]"
May 27, 1920   "An Old Novel [Charlotte Ogle]"
June 17, 1920   Review of *The Mills of the Gods* (Robins)

British Male Novelists and Novels

(rediscovered essays)

Jan. 4, 1905   Review of *Next-Door Neighbours* (Ridge)
March 17, 1905   "Barham of Beltana [W.E. Norris]"
March 31, 1905   Review of *The Fortunes of Farthings* (Dawson)
May 17, 1905   Review of *Arrows of Fortune* (A. Gissing)
Oct. 27, 1905   Review of *The Letter Killeth* (Inchbold)
Nov. 1, 1905   Review of *Lone Marie* (W.E. Norris)
Nov. 1, 1905   Review of *The Devil's Due* (Burgin)
Dec. 13, 1905   "'Delta'"
March 9, 1906   Review of *The House of Shadows* (Farrer)
Apr. 13, 1906   Review of *The Face of Clay* (Vachell)
June 22, 1906   Review of *Mrs. Grundy's Crucifix* (V. Brown)
Feb. 13, 1907   "*The Private Papers of Henry Ryecroft*"
Feb. 22, 1907   Review of *Temptation* (Bagot)
Sept. 6, 1907   Review of *The New Religion* (Maartens)
Feb. 6, 1908   Review of *Somehow Good* (DeMorgan)
Jan. 11, 1912   "The Novels of George Gissing"
July 26, 1917   "*Lord Jim*"
Sept. 20, 1917   "Mr. Conrad's 'Youth'"
March 14, 1918   "Mr. Conrad's Crisis"
Sept. 15, 1918   "A Practical Utopia [Oliver Onions]"
Feb. 13, 1919   "Small Talk About Meredith"
March 27, 1919   "Dickens by a Disciple"
Dec. 18, 1919   "Memories of Meredith"
July 15, 1920   "A Disillusioned Romantic [Conrad]"
March 3, 1921   "A Prince of Prose [Conrad]"
Apr. 28, 1921   "Scott's Character"
June 30, 1923   "An Impression of Gissing"
Nov. 17, 1923   "Mr. Bennett and Mrs. Brown"--Early version
Apr. 11, 1925   "The Two Samuel Butlers"
March 20, 1926   Review of *The Days of Dickens* (Hayward)
Feb. 11, 1928   Review of *Memories and Notes* (Hope)

Poetry and Poets
(rediscovered essays)

Apr. 21, 1906   "Poets' Letters"
June 15, 1906   "Wordsworth and the Lakes"
May 31, 1907   "Philip Sidney"
Apr. 2, 1908   "Wordsworth Letters"
Nov. 2, 1916   "Among the Poets"
May 27, 1917   "The Perfect Language"
Aug. 16, 1917   "John Davidson"
Aug. 23, 1917   "A Victorian Echo"
March 21, 1918   "Swinburne Letters"
May 1, 1918   "Two Irish Poets"
May 30, 1918   "Dreams and Realities"
Aug. 29, 1918   "The Sad Years"
Oct. 10, 1918   "Adventurers All"
Oct. 31, 1918   "The Candle of Vision"
June 20, 1919   "Is This Poetry? [T.S. Eliot, J.M. Murry]"
Nov. 21, 1919   "Maturity and Immaturity"
Dec. 11, 1919   "Watts-Dunton's Dilemma"
Jan. 19, 1924   Review of *The Poems of Lord Herbert of
                   Cherbury* (G.C.M. Smith, ed.)
Feb. 16, 1924   Review of *Unpublished Letters of Matthew
                   Arnold* (Whitridge, ed.)
Apr. 21, 1928   "Mr. Yeats"

· *Drama and Theater*
(rediscovered essays)

Apr. 18, 1906   "The Poetic Drama"
Apr. 20, 1911   "Rachel"
Oct. 31, 1918   "Abraham Lincoln"
June 6, 1919   "On Some of the Old Actors"
Oct. 16, 1919   "Landor in Little"
Apr. 17, 1920   "The Higher Court"
July 15, 1920   "Pure English"
July 24, 1920   "The Cherry Orchard"
Apr. 2, 1921   "Congreve"
Aug. 23, 1924   "Editions-de-Luxe"
Oct. 18, 1924   "Restoration Comedy"
Apr. 11, 1925   Review of *Guests and Memories* (Taylor)
Apr. 25, 1925   Review of *A Player Under Three Reigns*
                   (Forbes Robertson)
Oct. 17, 1925   "Congreve [Review of *Comedies by William
                   Congreve* (Dobrée, ed.)]"
Apr. 28, 1928   Review of *Behind the Scenes with Cyril
                   Maude*
June 30, 1928   Review of *On the Stage* (Arliss)
Nov. 17, 1928   "Plays ..."

Other Arts

(rediscovered essays)

Apr. 24, 1909	"The Opera"--no chart
Aug. 5, 1909	"Art and Life"
Jan. 9, 1920	"Pictures and Portraits"
Apr. 23, 1921	"Ethel Smyth"
May 9, 1925	Review of *The Tragic Life of Vincent Van Gogh* (Piérard)
Aug. 15, 1925	Review of *Time, Taste, and Furniture* (Warne)
Oct. 17, 1925	Review of *Twenty Years of My Life* (Jopling-Rowe)
Dec. 5, 1925	"Melba"
1926	"Julia Margaret Cameron"
July 14, 1928	Review of *Clara Butt: Her Life Story* (Ponder)
February 1930	"Recent Paintings by Vanessa Bell: ... Foreword"
March 1934	" ... Recent Paintings by Vanessa Bell: ... Foreword"

History, Geography, Sociology

(rediscovered essays)

Dec. 6, 1905	"A Description of the Desert"
Aug. 11, 1906	"Trafficks and Discoveries [Review of *English Voyages of the Sixteenth Century* (Raleigh)]"
Oct. 3, 1906	"Portraits of Places"
July 30, 1908	"The Stranger in London"
Dec. 3, 1908	"A Vanished Generation"
Jan. 7, 1909	"Venice"
Apr. 15, 1909	"Gentlemen Errant"
June 29, 1916	"Past and Present at the English Lakes"
Nov. 9, 1916	"London Revisited"
Dec. 21, 1916	"Social Life in England"
March 29, 1917	"The House of Lyme"
May 10, 1917	"A Cambridge V.A.D."
Dec. 12, 1918	"Trafficks and Discoveries"
Jan. 9, 1919	"The War from the Street"
Oct. 25, 1924	Review of *Richard Hakluyt* (F. Watson)
Oct. 25, 1924	Review of *Smoke Rings and Roundelays* (W. Partington, comp.)
Aug. 8, 1925	Review of *Unknown Essex* (Maxwell)
Dec. 5, 1925	Review of *Some of the Smaller Manor Houses of Sussex* (Wolesley)
Dec. 26, 1925	Review of *From Hall-Boy to House-Steward* (Lanceley)
March 6, 1926	Review of *Paradise in Piccadilly* (Furniss)
March 27, 1926	Review of *Steeple-Jacks and Steeplejacking* (Larkins)
March 5, 1927	Review of *The Immortal Isles* (Gordon)
Feb. 25, 1928	Review of *The Cornish Miner* (Jenkin)
March 1932	"Great Men's Houses"

Asian and Russian Literature
(rediscovered essays)

May 1, 1913	"Chinese Stories"
Feb. 1, 1917	"Tolstoy's 'The Cossacks'"
Oct. 11, 1917	"A Minor Dostoevsky"
May 16, 1918	"Tchehov's Questions"
Oct. 24, 1918	"Valery Brussof"
Dec. 19, 1918	"The Russian View"
Aug. 7, 1920	"Gorky on Tolstoi"
July 1925	"The Tale of Genji"

French Literature
(rediscovered essays)

Aug. 7, 1913	Review of *Les Copains* (Romains)
May 3, 1924	Review of *Anatole France* (May)
July 5, 1924	"Stendhal"
1925	"Stendhal [Review of *La Vie de Henri Bru-lard*]"
Feb. 13, 1929	"On Not Knowing French"

Biography, Individual and Collective [By Others]
(rediscovered essays)

Feb. 2, 1911	"The Duke and Duchess of Newcastle-upon-Tyne"
Nov. 29, 1917	"Stopford Brooke"
Dec. 20, 1917	"Rebels and Reformers"
Aug. 13, 1920	"A Character Sketch"
Feb. 9, 1924	Review of *Glimpses of Authors* (Ticknor)
June 21, 1924	Review of *The Life and Last Words of Wilfrid Ewart* (S. Grahame)
Apr. 11, 1925	Review of *Mainly Victorian* (Ellis)
May 16, 1925	Review of *Celebrities of Our Time* (Bern--stein)
June 3, 1925	"John Addington Symonds"
Nov. 14, 1925	"Saint Samuel of Fleet Street"

Autobiography and Memoirs

(rediscovered essays)

Aug. 29, 1906	"The English Mail Coach"
1908	"The Sunset" ...'the life of Leslie Stephen by a member of his household'"
Oct. 12, 1916	"'The Fighting Nineties'"
Apr. 12, 1917	"In Good Company"
Dec. 20, 1917	"Sunset Reflections"
June 27, 1918	"A Victorian Socialist"
Dec. 19, 1918	"A View of the Russian Revolution"
June 28, 1923	"Sir Thomas Browne"
Feb. 16, 1924	"Arthur Yates: An Autobiography"

May 10, 1924   "Mr. Benson's Memories"
June 5, 1924   Review of *Days That Are Gone* (de Sales
                    la Terriere)
June 21, 1924   Review of *Unwritten History* (C. Hamilton)
June 21, 1924   Review of *Robert Smith Surtees*
July 12, 1924   Review of *Before the Mast--and After*
                    (Runciman)
July 19, 1924   Review of *The Truth at Last* (Hawtrey)
Nov. 8, 1924   Review of *Peggy: The Story of One Score*
                    Years and Ten (Webling)
March 28, 1925   Review of *This for Remembrance* (Lord
                    Coleridge)
Apr. 18, 1925   Review of *Further Reminiscences* (Baring-
                    Gould)
Aug. 8, 1925   Review of *In My Anecdotage* (Elliot)
Sept. 26, 1925   "Life of Sir Francis Darwin"--no chart
Oct. 16, 1926   "Laughter and Tears"
Apr. 7, 1928   Review of *Stalky's Reminiscences* (Dun-
                    sterville)
May 5, 1928   Review of *Behind the Brass Plate* (Scho-
                    field)
Aug. 11, 1928   Review of *Day In, Day Out* (LeBlond)
Nov. 27, 1928   "Memories"

Letters and Diaries
(rediscovered essays)

Dec. 19, 1907   "William Allingham)
July 4, 1919   "Forgotten Benefactors"
Nov. 6, 1919   "Real Letters"

Humor and Whimsy
(rediscovered essays)

March 18, 1917   "Parodies"
June 20, 1918   "Loud Laughter"
June 4, 1921   "Trousers"
Dec. 15, 1921   "Fantasy"
July 3, 1924   "The Week End"

Personal Essays [By Others]
(rediscovered essays)

Dec. 14, 1916   "Old and Young"
Feb. 8, 1917   "Melodious Meditations"
Dec. 27, 1917   "'The New Crusade'"
Jan. 17, 1918   "A Book of Essays"
May 23, 1918   "Imitative Essays"
July 17, 1919   "A Positivist"
Nov. 16, 1919   "The Limits of Perfection"
Dec. 23, 1920   "A Flying Lesson"
Feb. 12, 1927   "Victorian Jottings"

Literary Criticism [By Others]
(rediscovered essays)

Jan. 6, 1906	"A Nineteenth-Century Critic"
Jan. 25, 1906	Review of *The Author's Progress* (Lorimer)
Dec. 21, 1916	"Mr. Symons's Essays"
Jan. 18, 1917	"Romance"
June 7, 1917	"Creative Criticism"
Sept. 6, 1917	"To Read or Not to Read"
Oct. 25, 1917	"Hearts of Controversy"
Nov. 14, 1918	"Mr. Howells on Form"
Nov. 21, 1918	"Bad Writers"
Oct. 2, 1919	"Mr. Gosse and His Friends"
Feb. 24, 1921	"Henley's Criticism"
Sept. 27, 1924	"Appreciations"
July 3, 1926	"Romance and the 'Nineties"
July 1930	"The Essays of Augustine Birrell"

Literary Theory--Not Reviews
(rediscovered essays)

Feb. 25, 1905	"The Decay of Essay-Writing"
1922	"Byron and Mr. Briggs"
October 1926	"How Should One Read a Book?"--Early version
Summer 1927	"What Is a Novel?"
May 15, 1928	"Preferences ... "
April 1929	"The 'Censorship' of Books"
1930	"Three Characters"
1940	"Anon"
1941	"The Reader"

Familiar Essays by Virginia Stephen Woolf
(rediscovered essays; no charts)

March 1905	"Street Music"
July 19, 1905	"An Andalusian Inn"
July 26, 1905	"A Priory Church"
Aug. 16, 1905	"The Value of Laughter"
Dec. 28, 1905	"A Walk by Night"
Aug. 15, 1916	"Heard on the Downs"
Apr. 25, 1919	"The Eccentrics"
July 23, 1930	"The Plumage Bill"
Apr. 5, 1924-	
Sept. 5, 1925	"From Alpha to Omega" (a compendium)
[*passim*]	

1942-Present

When she died, only fifty-two of Virginia Woolf's essays were available in the two *Common Reader* collections (1925, 1932). Of these, most had been published before, in variant forms, in periodicals; while ten were "new"-- that is, written by her specifically for either *The Common Reader* or *The Common Reader: Second Series* (usually called *The Second Common Reader*).

For some of the "new" essays, however, Woolf used parts of earlier book reviews, adapting titles, copying out passages and inserting them in the right places, meanwhile returning to the same or similar sources and starting afresh, from a different angle. Such an essay, for example, is "The Elizabethan Lumber Room" in *Common Reader I*, based partly on (uncollected) reviews written originally for the *TLS* ("Trafficks and Discoveries" [Dec. 12, 1918], "Richard Hakluyt" [Oct. 25, 1924], and "Sir Thomas Browne" [June 28, 1923]).

"One of the most elaborate show-pieces of biographical criticism" in her early period, thinks Edward Hungerford,[1] was a review mentioned above (p. 11): "The Duke and Duchess of Newcastle-upon-Tyne" (*TLS*, Feb. 2, 1911). When adapted for *Common Reader I*, it suffered a sea-change similar to that which would later overtake Woolf's hero in her 1929 novel *Orlando* during a voyage: its subject became wholly feminine. From being an essay about a famous man and his equally famous wife, it concentrated on the wife only, and "The Duchess of Newcastle" was born, in the course of which Woolf dropped some quotations from the Duchess' writings used before, and added new ones. Both essays are worthwhile.

Sometimes the carryover between former review and new piece in the *Common Reader* is slight. "The Russian View" (*TLS*, Dec. 19, 1918) contributes part of a title and a quotation from Hagbert Wright to the new "The Russian Point of View." But its subjects, two minor Slavic authors, have little in common with the exalted triumvirate of the new *Common Reader* essay: Chekhov, Dostoevsky and Tolstoi--the Chekhovian part of which Woolf had meanwhile had a chance to brew in two reviews of his short stories, 1918-19.[2] Assessments of Dostoevsky's *The Gambler* and Tolstoy's *The Cossacks* (*TLS*, Oct. 11 and Feb 1, 1917, respectively) also contributed to "The Russian Point of View." While "On Not Knowing Greek," another new essay in *Common Reader I*, had enjoyed a partial forerunner in "The Perfect Language" (*TLS*, May 24, 1917).

Reminders of earlier items are harder to find in the "new" essays written specially for *Common Reader II*. By that time (1932) Woolf was writing less often for the *TLS* or, for that matter, any journal, and her approach to compiling a collection seems to have been different.

After Virginia's death, Leonard Woolf began issuing other collections of her essays, beginning in 1942 with *The Death of the Moth* and continuing through 1958 with three others: *The Moment* (1947), *The Captain's Death Bed* (1950), and *Granite and Rainbow* (1958). Some of their contents--a total of 111 essays--were new items found in manuscript by Leonard Woolf; but most had been published before.

In 1965, Jean Guiguet edited a group of forty-six pieces written during the busy years 1918-20, called *Contemporary Writers*, and in 1976 Mary Lyon another forty-six in *Books and Portraits*. (For purposes of compilation here, I omit Leonard's ambitious project, begun in 1966 and carried through 1967: the four volumes of *Collected Essays*, which were meant to duplicate in a different order the contents of the *Common Readers* and the four posthumous collections he himself had edited, but which actually omitted a few items.)

The London Scene, five pieces originally published in *Good Housekeeping* (London), 1931-32, was printed in 1975. *Women and Writing* (1979), edited by Michele Barrett, despite its promising title, included only three items not collected already.

Meanwhile some essays still in manuscript were on the move. *Adam International Review* (1972) printed two, charts for both of which are included in the present study. Finally, two manuscript essays, "Anon" and "Reading" appeared in the Fall-Winter (1979) issue of *Twentieth Century Literature*, preceded by the equally impressive "Byron and Mr. Briggs" in *The Yale Review* (March 1979). All have a place in this volume.

In 1957, a year before *Granite and Rainbow*, edited by Leonard Woolf, came out, B[rownlee] J[ean] Kirkpatrick published the first official *Bibliography* of Virginia Woolf's works,[3] including all of the articles, collected and uncollected, known at the time to have been written by her. Ms. Kirkpatrick, however, in her "Preface" to this first edition, noted: "It is likely that Virginia Woolf contributed anonymously to the *Speaker*, which ceased publication in 1907, and to the *Guardian* between 1904 and 1907. It has not been possible to record these contributions as the marked files have not been located."[4] As a result, the first essay listed in 1957 was "Literary Geography" (*TLS*, March 10, 1905)--although "Street Music," *National Review*, "1905," third on the list, was actually the first of those at hand: it came out in the March issue,

available presumably in February. Nor did she list "such
short unsigned notes [by Woolf] as appeared from time to
time in the *New Statesman and Nation* [sic; i.e., *Nation
and Athenaeum*] under the headings 'Books in Brief' and
'From Alpha to Omega'." (These omissions would be cor-
rected in Kirkpatrick's next edition.) In any case, the
total number of essays *and short stories* (about ten of
the latter) listed in 1957 was 375.

     A decade later, by 1967, when the second edition of
the *Bibliography* emerged,[5] the number was upped consider-
ably. Not only had fifty items under "Books in Brief"
and "From Alpha to Omega" in the *Nation and Athenaeum*
been added, but the early 1905 diary volume kept by Virginia and now in the Berg Collection, New York Public Library, had been consulted and its contents noted. "In
the diary Virginia Woolf often indicated the author or
title of the book reviewed, or of the essay title, as well
as the periodical to which the contribution had been sent.
Sometimes, however, her information was less detailed;
this has meant that not all the contributions she noted
in the diary have been traced," Ms. Kirkpatrick explained.[6]
"There are, undoubtably [sic], further early unsigned contributions to the *Guardian*, the *Speaker*, and possibly the
Outlook...." Untraced items were noted in an Appendix to [7]
Section C ("Contributions to Periodicals and Newspapers").
In any case, the total basic list of essays (including
"letters to the editor") and short stories numbered now,
in the second edition, about 465, or ninety more than before.

     To a true bibliographer, the "untraced items" pre-
sented of course a challenge--a challenge met full-face
by scholar Suzanne Henig, then working on her dissertation
for New York University. Scanning the periodical files
herself, she came up with solid data on three items which
Ms. Kirkpatrick, in connection with the list referred to
above, had asked for help on: "The Feminine Note in Fiction," "A Priory Church," and "The Value of Laughter."
Other researchers also offered input and the result was a
third edition of the *Bibliography* with fuller notations
than ever, published in 1980.[8]

     In this, the current edition of "Kirkpatrick" availa-
ble to scholars, fifty-eight more reviews, "most of which
are unsigned,"[9] were added, bringing the total under "Contributions to Periodicals and Newspapers" to over five
hundred items. In the Preface Ms. Kirkpatrick expresses
her certainty that there are still more out there lurking;
nor has she dispensed with a list of "Doubtful and Untraced
Contributions."[10] (How the present study has used this
list will be seen in Chapter 4.)

Keeping in mind B.J. Kirkpatrick's dedication to an
ever-burgeoning task down the years, yet the enormous
amount of reading which Virginia Woolf did for her wide-
ranging book reviews and essays could hardly be suggested
in a traditional bibliography. Thus the need for something like Brenda Silver's admirable *Virginia Woolf's Reading Notebooks* (1983)[11] which combined quotations from
Woolf's copious reading notebooks, dating from 1905 on,
with bibliographical data for the various entries, data
scantily supplied by Virginia herself--and understandably,
since the notebooks represented her own personal workshop.
Now the University of Sussex Library is microfilming,[12] for
scholars' use, its half of the sixty-seven notebooks,
verbatim. Such materials as these and Professor Silver's
study enable us to realize (for the number of essays they
cover--some thirty percent of the total composed) the
energy of Virginia Woolf's approach as she wrote and re-
wrote, often many times, her responses to biography and
memoirs, travel books, poetry, drama and fiction; and produced in the process some of the most rewarding essays in
the canon of English literature.

Notes for Chapter 1

1904-41

1. (1942). In Kronenberger, *The Republic of Letters*.
New York: Knopf, 1955. P. 245.

2. Goldman, p. 356. The essay referred to is Woolf,
"Madame de Sévigné," in *The Death of the Moth*, ed. by Leonard Woolf. London: Hogarth; New York: Harcourt, Brace,
1942. P. 40.

3. August 18, 1921. In Virginia Woolf, *Diary*, Vol.
II, ed. by Anne Olivier Bell. London: Hogarth; New York:
Harcourt Brace Jovanovich, 1978. Pp. 132-33.

4. October 7, 1939. In Virginia Woolf, *Diary*, Vol. V,
ed. by Anne Olivier Bell. London: Hogarth; New York: Harcourt Brace Jovanovich, 1984. P. 241.

5. See Preface, note 4, above (*infra*).

6. Henig, p. 6.

7. Written in response to an essay by a Mrs. Lathbury
in the journal *The Nineteenth Century*, the article is dated
Sept. 8, 1880. Owned in MS by Washington State University,
it will be printed, for the first time, in Julia Stephen,
Stories for Children, Essays for Adults, ed. by Diane Gil-
lespie and Elizabeth Steele (Syracuse, N.Y.: Syracuse University Press, 1987).

8. Quentin Bell, *Virginia Woolf, A Biography*, Vol.
II. London: Hogarth; New York: Harcourt Brace Jovanovich,
1972. P. 87. For Kitty Maxse's early help, see Woolf,
diary, Jan. 16, 1905 (note 10 below).

9. Henig, p. 7.

10. Feb. 8, 1905. This early diary, in the Berg Collection of the New York Public Library, is one of nine
such diaries (1897-1909 *passim*) to be published soon under
the editorship of Professor Mitchell A. Leaska; quotation
till then is restricted.

11. Robert Steven Ferebee, *Virginia Woolf as an Essayist*. (University of New Mexico, 1981). Ann Arbor, Mich.:
University Microfilms, 1982. P. 106.

12. Henig, p. 21.

13. Ferebee, p. 4.

14. Hungerford, p. 33.

15. In Virginia Woolf, *Letters*, Vol. I, ed. by Nigel
Nicolson and Joanne Trautmann. [British title: *The Flight
of the Mind*]. London: Hogarth; New York: Harcourt Brace
Jovanovich, 1975. P. 421.

16. Hungerford, p. 43.

17. *Letters*, Vol. II, ed. by Nigel Nicolson and Joanne
Trautmann. [British title: *The Question of Things Happen-
ing*]. London: Hogarth; New York: Harcourt Brace Jovanovich,
1976. P. 67.

18. Hungerford, p. 75.

19. Henig, p. 43.

20. Hungerford, p. 138.

21. *Ibid.*, p. 139.

22. *Ibid.*, pp. 126-27.

23. *The New Republic* published about thirty articles
of hers, beginning in 1923 and ending in 1940. Some were
printed *only* in the *NR*.

24. Henig, pp. 169-70.

25. Ferebee, pp. 244-45.

Variety of Topics

1. Hungerford, p. 79.

2. Lehmann, p. 100.

3. Ferebee, p. 17.

4. Early diary (see note 10 above).

5. Hungerford, p. 27.

6. Henig, p. 242.

7. Hungerford, p. 114.

8. *Ibid.*, p. 46.

9. *Ibid.*, pp. 93-94.

10. London: Hogarth, 1965.   Pp. 159-60.

11. Hyman, p. 107.

12. Ferebee, pp. 17, 213-40 *passim*.

1942-Present

1. Hungerford, p. 40.

2. The second such review, "The Russian Background" (1919), is reprinted in *Books and Portraits*, ed. by Mary Lyon. London: Hogarth, 1977; New York: Harcourt Brace Jovanovich, 1978. Pp. 123-25.

3. *A Bibliography of Virginia Woolf*. London: Rupert Hart-Davis, 1957.

4. *Ibid.*, p. ix.

5. *A Bibliography of Virginia Woolf*. 2nd ed., rev. London: Rupert Hart-Davis, 1967.

6. *Ibid.*, p. ix.

7. *Ibid.*, pp. 95-130; Appendix, pp. 130-31.

8. *A Bibliography of Virginia Woolf*. 3rd ed. Oxford: Clarendon, 1980.

9. *Ibid.*, p. ix.

10. *Ibid.*, pp. 178-81.

11. Princeton, N.J.: Princeton University Pr., 1983. Virginia Woolf's reading technique is apparent from her advice to Vita Sackville-West, who was perusing a memoirist: "[T]ry reading as if you were catching a swarm of bees, not hunting down one dart[-]like dragon fly." ([June 1, 1926]. *Letters*, Vol. III, ed. by Nigel Nicolson and Joanne Trautmann. [British title: *A Change of Perspective*]. London: Hogarth, 1977; New York: Harcourt Brace Jovanovich, 1978. P. 268.)

12. The other half, except for a set of reading notes on primary sources of the collected essay "Oliver Goldsmith" (1934), belong to the Henry W. and Albert A. Berg Collection, New York Public Library (Astor, Lenox and Tilden Foundations). The Goldsmith notes are owned by Yale University (Beinecke Library).

Chapter 2

A GARLAND OF PASSAGES BY VIRGINIA WOOLF

Assessments of Some Who Made Their Living by the Pen

These passages, printed in different times and different places during a career that lasted almost forty years, are presented to show the quality of the rediscovered essays:--

She was never a revelation to the young, a stern comrade, a brilliant and extravagantly admired friend, a writer whose sentences sang in one's brain and were half absorbed into one's blood. And directly one has set down any of the above phrases one is conscious of the irony with which she would have disclaimed any such wish or intention. ("Jane AUSTEN," 1913)

BYRON was a fine bold boy and wrote far better letters from abroad than his people had a right to expect. He should have stayed an undergraduate for ever, dominating his own group but strictly kept in order ... ; also here are women; and he must needs be a man of the world, and learn the trade from that tight lipped hard faced prosaic peeress Lady Melbourne who soon brought out the worst of him--the dancing master and dandy, so proud of his conquests though so obviously ashamed of his foot.... The big boy who limped off the field in a rage because he had been clean bowled for two or three runs needed what women call "managing". But what woman could give it him? He was dangerous; a treacherous lap dog. In the midst of sentiment down came the sledge hammer of fact. Who could be more unflinching and direct? ("Byron and Mr. Briggs," 1922)

There is no need for the modern reader to put himself into
a strained attitude in reading him. He need be no more
licentious, no more hearty, no more fond of oaths and
horseplay than he is by nature. To appreciate CONGREVE
one need not be much different from what one is--only better. ("Congreve," 1925)

Let any one who has spent his life in writing novels consider the day which has now arrived for George GISSING.
The fruit of his life stands before us--a row of red volumes. If they were biographies, histories, books about
books even, or speculations upon money or the course of
the world there would be no need for the peculiar shudder.
But they bear titles like these--"Denzil Quarrier," "Born
in Exile," "New Grub Street"; places and people that have
never existed save in one brain now cold. They are only
novels. It seems that there is genuine cause for shudder-
ing when one's work takes this form. Dead leaves cannot
be more brittle or more worthless than things faintly
imagined--and that the fruit of one's life should be
twelve volumes of dead leaves! We have one moment of
such panic before the novels of George Gissing, and then
we rise again. Not in our time will they be found worthless. ("The Novels of George Gissing," 1912)

If this were the age of faith, Dr. JOHNSON would certainly be Saint Samuel, Fleet Street would be full of holy
places where he preached his sermons and performed his
miracles.... Our age has somehow lost the art of making
haloes; but a man may fairly be said to be a Saint when
cabmen ... quote Johnson's sayings or invent Johnson's
sayings on a wet night in the Strand, as a writer in the
Times has lately heard them doing. Then, indeed, he has
eaten his way into the fabric of life and performs all the
functions of the gods, presiding over the fortunes of men,
and inspiring, albeit he wears a wig, a snuff-coloured
coat, rolls as he walks, and has a gluttonous appetite
for dinner. ("Saint Samuel of Fleet Street," 1925)

Anyone who wants to come near the character of SCOTT, or
to analyse the nature of his charm, must give full weight
to the fact that he spent hours every day during the
greater part of his life with the creatures of his imagination. The temperament which naturally indulges itself
thus is quite distinct from that which has no such bent....
When it came to writing he had merely to turn on the tap
and the accumulated resources rushed out. That this is
not the way in which the works of Flaubert were produced
is certain; but it is also probable that genius of a certain type must work unconsciously, like a natural force
which issues unchecked, almost unnoticed by its possessor.
To read Scott's life and not to see that he was perpetu-
ally under the sway of this power is to miss the flavour
and proportion of the whole. He had no say in the matter.
Whether he wrote well or ill, for money or for pleasure,
Scott was as much the slave of his imagination as a drunk-
ard is the slave of his dram.   ("Scott's Character," 1921)

Gazing from the gallery of some dismal gas-lit hall, one
has seen him, often enough, alert, slight, erect, as if
combating in his solitary person the forces of inertia
and stupidity massed in a sea upon the floor. On a near-
er glance, he appeared much of a knight-errant, candid,
indeed innocent of aspect; a Don Quixote born in the
Northern mists--shrewd, that is to say, rather than romantic. (*Re* George Bernard SHAW; "Pictures and Portraits,"
1920)

SPENSER sees at a distance. He sees Knights and ladies
with regret, with desire, but not with belief. There is
no sharpness in his figures; no edge; no anguish; no sin
.... On the other hand he shows us ... the world surround-
ing them. He realizes time and change. And looking back,
from a distance he sees them pictorially; grouped like the
figures in a fresco, with the flowers growing at their
feet, behind them marble pillars, trees with bright birds,
and the libbard and the lion roaming or couchant. There

is no tension; no direction; but always movement, as the metre flings its curve of sound, to break, like a wave on the same place, and like a wave to withdraw, to fill a-gain. Folded in this incantation we drowse and sleep; yet always see through the waters, something irradiated. Spenser standing on the threshold ... is half in shadow, half in light. Half is still unrealised for he cannot confine emotions within himself. He must symbolise, ex-teriorise. Jealousy is not a passion to issue on actual lips. He must float it outwards; make it abstract; give it a symbolical shape. He cannot speak through the mouths of individuals. The body containing within it-self all the passions is still sunk in shadow. But the other half is in the light. He is aware of his art....
("Anon," 1940)

Every one writing on STENDHAL compares him with a man of science, but the comparison, if we impute coolness to the scientist, is entirely misleading. Passion, as well as interest in passion, a dry but pervasive heat, some obdur-acy and angularity of mental temperament, give this sur-geon's investigations a character far removed from the impersonality of a truly scientific proceeding. ("Sten-dhal,"1925)

[I]t is as easy for him to see heaven in the earth as to see grass and stone there. Indeed, his quiet assumption that not only mountains, trees, and lakes, but the most minute changes of leaf and herb, are the seriously import-ant things in all lives, amusing as it is at first, per-suades us in the end that it is, or should be, really so. For in WORDSWORTH's eyes this spectacle of the country-side which we find variously pleasant or delightful as a relief from other things is the most solemn truth that exists. It is no mere curiosity or a taste for the pic-turesque that drives him to walk out among the hills, and to know all that can be known about the things that grow there. Rather he is trying to read the signs which, what-ever their meaning, are to him never made in vain.
("Wordsworth and the Lakes," 1906)

Chapter 3

FOCUS OF THIS STUDY

The Purpose of the Charts

As William York Tindall says about Virginia Woolf's essays, in his *Forces in Modern British Literature* (1947): "Haste and imperfection ... are no part of her work."[1]

She devoted as much time to her reviews as to her other writings. This dedication was evident from the first. In a Diary entry for February 18, 1905 she exclaimed: "It takes me almost as long to rewrite one page, as to write four fresh ones...."[2] And exactly seventeen years later, in 1922: "[W]hen I write a review I write every sentence as if it were going to be tried before 3 [*sic*] Chief Justices...."[3]

Her husband testifies to this care in his preface to her posthumous collection of essays *The Death of the Moth* (1942). "I do not think that Virginia Woolf ever contributed any article to any paper which she did not write and rewrite several times." He mentions finding a typescript of a review that had "no fewer than eight or nine complete revisions ... which she had herself typed out."

Obviously her process of composing was not as simple as it seems on the surface, when one reads the finished product. Six decades ago the idea of the "Common Reader" was borrowed by Woolf from Samuel Johnson and became an idealized figure with whom she personally identified. Though self-educated, like Woolf herself, the Common Reader is a critic of worthwhile opinions, dwelling anywhere on the globe.

In the preface to her first collection of essays, she describes this figure to "explain ... her title," as Mark Goldman says, and thus provide "a statement of purpose."[4] As depicted by her, the Common Reader wishes to construct from his/her reading "some kind of whole--[1] a portrait of a man, [2] a sketch of an age, [3] a theory of the art of writing."[5] S/he does not, however, wish to be an "expert." Thus in speaking herself to the "Common Reader," Virginia Woolf took care not to expose overtly what Edward Hungerford calls "the technicalities of scholarship,"[6] her own or anyone else's. While this makes for a more graceful style, in a sense it was unfortunate, since it led to some downgrading of her talent among scholars, then and now.

*Virginia Woolf's Literary Sources and Allusions: A
Guide to the Essays* (1973), mentioned earlier, attempted
to correct this impression for the collected essays. The
present volume hopes to do the same for the uncollected
ones--soon to be incorporated in the six volumes of complete essays forecast in the preface.

Here as before, the charts following (in Chapter 4)
have been prepared as a double service to readers--to doc-
ument, one, Woolf's wide breadth of reading and, two, the
care she put into shaping her essays.

Both aspects are considered in the paragraphs below.

Reading the Charts for Bibliography

The reader has probably gathered that, both in her
reading notebooks and in the essays themselves, Woolf's
handling of bibliographical details tended to be casual.
Such casualness extended even to the collected essays,
for which there were few footnotes (and some of those were
wrong) and of course no bibliographies. The uncollected
essays are a slightly different matter for the reader.
At least for a published review, one can count on having
the title and author of the book reviewed, printed at the
top or bottom--only the *Cornhill* was sometimes careless
in this regard.

But identification of the primary source or impulse
of a piece is merely the beginning when considering a
longer, more complex uncollected essay. Woolf may have
felt that to be specific about sources and allusions
within the text itself, would spoil her flow of argument.
While including such details occasionally, she obviously
does not consider them vital to the reader's enjoyment,
and to an extent, of course, she is right. Also relevant
is her apparent belief that her audience of Common Readers were well educated in the lore, titles and authors of
Western, and especially English, literature. She may
have carried this concept too far, as reviewer Marghanita
Laski's wail when the *Collected Essays* came out suggests:
"What kind of A-level candidates does the Hogarth Press
think we are?"

Whatever the reason, few of the essays are without
their challenge for the questing reader. Virginia Woolf's
sources range from the familiar or obvious, to the unusual
or esoteric, as do the ways in which she employed them.
By supplying, so to speak, the footnotes she herself omitted, the following charts are meant to reassure the reader
that Virginia Woolf, as scholar, stood on solid ground.

Reading the Charts for Essay Structure

The presence of sources for and allusions in the
essays leads naturally to the question of form in the
individual essay--writer's intention and reader's per-
ception both viewed from a structural standpoint. This
feature is codified in the charts also.

Analyzing an essay structurally is another way of
illuminating one aspect of Woolf's works that cannot be
over-emphasized: her diversity of approach. Virginia
Woolf wrote criticism to no pre-determined formula. The
pose she assumes of coming to each work for the first
time was actually no pose. Her appraisal of a work of
art was as spontaneous as anyone with a wide reading
background like hers could hope to achieve.

In general, each chart follows the outline described
below--wherein four categories, (1) Main Source, (2) Supportive Source(s), (3) Important Allusion(s) and (4) Passing Allusion(s), are presented for every essay when they
occur.

   (1) Main Sources generally are described in one of
       two ways:

       (a) "Obvious Source(s)"--indicated editorially,
           outside the body of the piece (common in the
           uncollected essays);

       (b) "Inferred Source(s)"--indicated within the
           body of the essay, whether covertly (e.g.,
           as in "John Davidson": "Mr. Fineman sends
           us back to Davidson's books" [Davidson's
           books being the inferred source]) or overtly
           (e.g., by title).

A "Stated Impulse" is a Main Source stated editorially,
outside the essay, but which is not in fact the main
source, rather a jumping-off point. This can happen when
Woolf, given something to review, prefers to discuss
another work or works by the same author. (See, e.g.,
"The Novels of George Gissing," supposed to be a review
of eight specific titles by that writer, but leaning heav-
ily on four other Gissing works instead.)

   (2) "Supportive Source(s)"--related works Woolf used
in researching her topic--whether internally indicated or
used without identification are almost as germane to the
essay's argument and structure as category (1). In the
case of the "idea" piece--especially literary theory--
when the governing thesis of the essay itself is the main-
stem, or in a review of a live piece of theater seen as
entertainment, there can be no other *than* "Supportive
Source(s)."

(3) "Important Allusion(s)" highly enrich the argument but are not necessary to its support.

(4) "Passing Allusion(s)" provide graceful tracery that gives the growth its final outline. Marginal comparisons and contrasts, facts and names far from vital to the essay's argument, are introduced here. This is where one would start if one were pruning the essay.

N.B.: A "pecking order" exists in regard to authors' names. For example, if the author of a work is listed under "Supportive Source(s)," his/her name will not appear below--though it may in fact fulfill both functions, in different parts of the essay. Likewise, an author's name under "Important Allusion(s)" will not normally appear in the "Passing" category.

An attempt has also been made, more consistently than in *Virginia Woolf's Literary Sources and Allusions*, to wed specific quotations to their sources by placing them immediately under the title(s) they belong to. This seems a better way of showing Virginia Woolf at work, choosing and ordering her materials.

For the writer, the literary scholar, the inquisitive reader, Virginia Woolf's collected essays have been, down the years, occasions of enlightenment and pleasure. It is their correlatives, the "uncollected" pieces, that *Virginia Woolf's Rediscovered Essays* tries to present, through a study of their literary sources and allusions. It is hoped that readers turning to the original texts with its aid will find them even more valuable than they might have otherwise.

Notes for Chapter 3

1. (1947). Vintage ed. New York: Vintage Books, 1956. P. 14.

2. Early diary (see Chapter 1, note 10, above).

3. February 18, 1922. *Diary*, Vol. II, ed. by Anne Olivier Bell. London: Hogarth; New York: Harcourt Brace Jovanovich, 1978. P. 169.

4. Goldman, p. 10.

5. Cf. her description of the "ordinary reader" in her longest collected essay, "Phases of Fiction" (orig. in *The Bookman* [New York], April-June 1929 *passim*; repr. in *Granite and Rainbow* and in Woolf, *Collected Essays*, Vol. II [pp. 56-57 espec.]).

6. Hungerford, p. 36.

7. "Lofty Intimations," *The Listener*, Oct. 20, 1967.

8. The rest of this chapter draws partly from parallel passages in *Virginia Woolf's Literary Sources and Allusions*, pp. 23-25.

Chapter 4

SOURCES AND ALLUSIONS USED

IN WRITING THE REDISCOVERED ESSAYS

Final Notes About the Charts

(1) The HEADING of each chart contains: (a) the title of the essay followed by (b) the year of composition
or, more often, of original publication; (c) the number
of the item as shown in B.J. Kirkpatrick's *Bibliography of
Virginia Woolf* -- 3rd edition; and finally, (d) the volume
title of reading notes, where applicable: numbers apply
to the Berg collection, New York Public Library, and letters to the Monks House Papers, University of Sussex.
(Omitted here *BUT FOUND IN APPENDIX A*, are the place and
exact date of original publication, further provenance of
the essay [if any], and indications of existing variants.)

(2) Within the charts themselves, in the case of
works with MORE THAN ONE EDITION: "Prob. ed." means either
that the edition(s) sought was/were unavailable, despite
diligent searching; or that the reading notes (where they
exist) contained no page numbers to aid the search. The
PLACE of publication is London unless otherwise shown.

(3) *Re* the fact, mentioned in many charts, that a
book is LISTED IN HOLLEYMAN (the catalogue of books owned
by Virginia and Leonard Woolf, published in 1975--for complete title see Appendix B, *infra*): this is meant to show
what works she had on hand or at least available when
writing, as she usually did, at home. But the Woolfs'
actual library was of course much larger, as G.A. Holleyman's Introduction emphasizes. The Woolfs themselves sold
or gave away many of their books; the Blitz destroyed others; and after Leonard's death, the executors of the estate rightly had first choice of the remainder. Thus,
"Holleyman" itself is necessarily incomplete. Not only
so but Holleyman and Treacher, Ltd., Brighton, had the
selling of only a portion of the Woolfs' library when,
bought by Washington State University, where it is now
housed, it passed from England to the United States. The
other half was purchased by Washington State at the same
time through the Bow Windows Bookshop, Lewes. And the
Bookshop did not issue a catalogue.

        Thus it seemed advisable to go to Pullman, Washing-
ton, as I first did in spring 1976, and compile a list of
the books there relating to literature which had belonged
to the Woolfs but were not covered in Holleyman. Later
learning that the Bow Windows Bookshop had sold another
batch of the Woolfs' books (formerly on loan to Leonard's
nephew Cecil Woolf for some years) to Washington State, I
went to Pullman again, in summer 1980. The "HOLLEYMAN
ADDENDUM" noted in the charts and included in *Virginia
Woolf's Literary Sources and Allusions: A Guide to the
Essays* as Appendix B, is the result. Since then, yet
another sixty titles were released in offer by Quentin
and Anne Olivier Bell. They appear in the present study
as Appendix B: "HOLLEYMAN ADDENDUM II." I am grateful to
Washington State University for keeping me abreast of its
acquisitions in this field.

        (4) Both Holleyman itself (though it does not list
publishers) and the Addenda have been helpful in assem-
bling the following charts. Equally useful--where READ-
ING NOTES were involved--is the superb study mentioned before: *Virginia Woolf's Reading Notebooks* by Brenda Silver.
It provides notes--where they exist--not only from Woolf's
basic sources, but also from the "extra works" composing
her reading environment: the "hidden springs" that fed
her imagination and increased her knowledge as she wrote.

        (5) As a rule--except where prompted by Brenda Sil-
ver's study--I have not collated the standard 18th- and
19th-century NOVELS mentioned in the essays, with Holleyman. Most of them are found there in profusion, and Woolf
had many other editions available to her, through the
British Museum and the London Library, both of which she
relied on to furnish her with books to supplement her own
holdings.

        (6) A word about the ESSAYS INCLUDED IN THIS STUDY.
Earlier I mentioned B.J. Kirkpatrick's list of "uncon-
firmed" essays, a list present in both the 2nd and 3rd
editions of the *Bibliography*. Such items in the 3rd edition number 47. Professor Suzanne Henig, whom Ms. Kirkpatrick mentions in her acknowledgments, was kind enough
to share with me copies of essays hard to find (particularly in the *Guardian*) thought to be by Virginia Woolf
and partially confirmed. My own researches and those of
others added more, with the result that I feel certain
enough about nine (out of the forty-seven) to add them to
the uncollected essays already specified in Ms. Kirkpatrick's principal list.

        An anomaly among the essays covered by this study is
"Great Men's Houses." Though collected in a small book
called *The London Scene* (New York: Frank Hallman, 1975),
it was inadvertently left out of *Virginia Woolf's Literary
Sources and Allusions*. It belongs in this compilation.

Two titles: "Mr. Bennett and Mrs Brown" and "How Should One Read a Book?" are so well known and often reprinted, that their presence again in this study may seem to be a mistake. But it is hard to imagine two pieces less like their final results. In each case we are dealing with something completely different between first instance and last. Hence this inclusion in their "uncollected" first forms.

Finally, four items appeared first not in journals or newspapers, but as parts of books: "Julia Margaret Cameron"; Virginia Stephen's short essay on her father included in Frederick Maitland's life of Sir Leslie; and two forewords to exhibition catalogues of paintings by Vanessa Bell (1930 and 1934). All pertain to family and will be included in the six-volume complete essays, to be issued starting soon.

COMPILATION

ABRAHAM LINCOLN (1918)   C130

Obvious Source:

John Drinkwater, *Abraham Lincoln*. Sidgwick and
Jackson, 1918.

Important Allusions:

Miscellaneous playwrights: Henrik Ibsen, William Shakespeare (mentioned by Drinkwater), Anton Tchehov

- -

ADVENTURERS ALL (1918)   C125

Obvious Sources:

(1) Muriel Stuart, *The Cockpit of Idols*.
Methuen, 1918.

Specific quote from: "The Cockpit of Idols."

Mentioned but not quoted from: "Heliodore."

(2) Aldous Huxley, *The Defeat of Youth and
Other Poems*. Oxford: Blackwell, 1918.

Specific quote from: "On the Bus."

Mentioned but not quoted from:

(a) "Social Amenities."

(b) "Topiary."

(3) Edith Sitwell, *Clowns' Houses*. Oxford:
Blackwell, 1918.

Specific quote from: "Déjeuner sur l'Herbe."

(4) *Songs for Sale. An Anthology of Recent Poetry*, ed. by E.B.C. Jones. Oxford: Blackwell, 1918.

Specific quote from: T.W. Earp, "Departure."

Mentioned but not quoted from: Frank Betts,
"The Pawns." (Orig. 1911)

AFTER HIS KIND (1906)   C3.2
                                         Reading notes
    Obvious Source: B1a

        M. Sturge Henderson, *After His Kind*. Duckworth,
        1905.

    Passing Allusions:

        (1) Mentioned by Henderson: Jane Austen

        (2) Don Quixote

- -

AN AMERICAN POET (1920)   C182.1

    Obvious Source:

        [Nicholas] Vachel Lindsay, *General William Booth
        Enters Into Heaven, and Other Poems*, w/intro-
        duction by Robert Nichols. Chatto and Windus,
        1919. (Orig. 1913)

        Specific quotes from:

        (1) "a short sermon"

            From "A Net to Snare the Moonlight" (1912)

        (2) "Mr. Lindsay recites the following"

            Ll. 1-11 from "General William Booth ..."
            (1912)

        (3) "rhetoric of the feeblest kind"

            From "To the United States Senate" (1911)

        (4) "little poem"

            "Look You, I'll Go Pray" (1910-12)

    Supportive Source:

        Lindsay, *The Chinese Nightingale*. New York:
        Macmillan, 1917.

        Specific quote from:

        "he will beat out his message"

        From "The Drunkard's Funeral" (1914)

Important Allusions (mentioned by Nichols):

Other works by Lindsay:

(1) *The Golden Book of Springfield.*   (Orig. 1920)

(2) *The Congo.*   (Orig. 1914)

- -

THE AMERICAN WOMAN (1905)   See pp. 178-79,
                                             KP
    Obvious Source:

        Elizabeth McCracken, *The Women of America.*   Mac-
        millan, 1905.

- -

AMONG THE POETS (1916)   C56

    Obvious Source:

        Stephen Coleridge, *An Evening in My Library
        Among the English Poets.*   Lane, 1916.

    Specific quotes from:

    (1) Obscure poets:

        (a) "a book of poems by a young American"

            Charles Henry Luders, *The Dead Nymph.*
            Charles Scribner's, 1892.

        (b) "an extract from a prize poem"

            Henry Hart Milman, "The Belvidere Apollo."
            (Orig. 1812)

    (2) Noted poets:

        (a) "a famous sonnet of Wordsworth's"

            William Wordsworth, "The World Is Too
            Much with Us."   (Orig. 1807)

        (b) Walt Whitman, "The Song of the Broad Axe."
            (Orig. 1855)

(c) "There is a line"

William Butler Yeats, "The Lake Isle of
Innisfree." (Orig. 1890)

Important Allusions:

(1) Miscellaneous poets (mentioned by S. Coleridge): Walter Savage Landor, James Russell
Lowell, John Masefield, Alexander Pope, Algernon Charles Swinburne

(2) George Bernard Shaw

Passing Allusions (mentioned by S. Coleridge):

(1) Obscure poets: Anne Reeves Aldritch, Lucy
Larcom

(2) Poems by Alfred Lord Tennyson:

(a) *In Memoriam*. (Orig. 1850)

(b) "Tears, Idle Tears" from *The Princess*.
(Orig. 1847)

- -

ANATOLE FRANCE (1924)   C246.11

Obvious Source:

James Lewis May, *Anatole France, the Man and
His Work*. Lane, 1924.

- -

ANON (1940; publ. in 1979)   Not in KP; ed.
                                        by Brenda Silver*
Supportive Sources:
                                        Reading notes #s
(1) "the historian says"   16, 21, and B2c

G.M. Trevelyan, *History of England*.+ Longmans, Green, 1926.

This is indicated by the reading notes (B2c)
and is listed in Holleyman.

(2) "the human voice sang too"; "their native
    tongue"

    E.K. Chambers and F. Sidgwick, eds., *Early*
    English Lyrics.+ Sidgwick and Jackson,
    1926.

    Poems XXXIII and IV, respectively; "woing"
    should read "wowing" and "no" should read
    "so."+

(3) "the scholars tell us"

    E.g., E.K. Chambers, *The Medieval Stage*.+
    2 vol. Oxford: Clarendon, 1903.

    This is indicated by the reading notes (#16).

(4) Sir Thomas Malory, *Le Morte DArthur* ... ,
    ed. by Sir Edward Strachey.+ Prob. ed.:
    Globe Ed. Macmillan, 1899. (Orig. publ.
    1485; in this ed. 1868)

    This is listed in Holleyman; it belonged to
    Leonard.

    Specific quotes from:

    (a) "They said" (p. 384)

        William Caxton, "Preface."+

    (b) 2nd quote (p. 384); "his bed" should
        read "her bed"+

    (c) "the peasants remember"

        Strachey, "Introduction."+

(5) "Harrison ... tells us" (p. 385)

    William Harrison, *Harrison's Description of*
    England in Shakspere's Youth, ed. by Fred-
    erick J. Furnivall. 2 vol. New Shakspere
    Society, 1877-1908. (Orig. 1577)

    This is indicated by the reading notes (#21)+
    and is listed in Holleyman Addendum.

    First quote, p. 386, is from here.

(6) Hugh Latimer, *Fruitfull Sermons*. Cotes,
    1635.

    This is indicated by the reading notes (#16)+
    and is listed in Holleyman.

Quotes 2-7, p. 386, and all quotes, pp.
387-88, are from here.

(7) "when Lady Ann Bacon writes to her son"

Poss. ed.:+ James Spedding, *The Letters and
the Life of Francis Bacon.* 7 vol. Longmans, Green, 1861-74. Espec. Vol. I.

Vols. 3-7 are listed in Holleyman; they belonged to Leslie Stephen. Vols. 1-2 are
listed in Holleyman Addendum II.

(8) "wrote Lady Ann Clifford"

The Diary of Lady Anne Clifford, ed. by
Vita Sackville-West. Heinemann, 1923.

This is listed in the reading notes (#16)+
and in Holleyman.

(9) "Pepys noted"

Sept. 2, 1666

Poss. ed.: Samuel Pepys, *Diaries and Correspondence*, ed. by Richard Lord Braybrooke.
6th ed. H.G. Bohn, 1849. (Orig. 1825)

This is listed in the reading notes (B2c)+
and in Holleyman.

(10) Edmund Spenser, *The Works of ...* , ed. by J.
Payne Collier. 5 vol. Bell and Daldy, 1862.

This is indicated by the reading notes (B2c)+
and is listed in Holleyman Addendum II; it
belonged to Leslie Stephen.

Specific quotes from:

(a) Collier, "The Life of Edmund Spenser."
Vol. I.

(i) Last 2 quotes, p. 389

(ii) First quote, p. 390

Spenser to Gabriel Harvey, Apr. 4,
1580

(b) Spenser, *The Faery Queen.* (Orig. 1590,
1596) Vols. I-IV.

(i) Last 2 quotes, p. 390

Book IV, Canto ii, Verses 32,
34; 2nd quote should start with
"infusion"

(ii) First quote, p. 392

Book III, Canto xii, Verse 5

(iii) 2nd quote, p. 392

"Mutability Cantos" [Book VII],
Canto vii, Verse 35

(11) Philip Henslowe, *Henslowe's Diary*, ed. by
Walter W. Greg.+   2 vol.   Bullen, 1904-08.

This is indicated by the reading notes (#16
and B2c).

2nd quote, p. 392, is from here.

(12) G[eorge] B[agshawe] Harrison, *Elizabethan
Plays and Players*.+   G. Routledge, 1940.

Last quote, p. 392, is from here (quoted by
Harrison):

Thomas Nashe, *Piers Penniless*.   (Orig. 1592)

(13) Christopher Marlowe, *Tamburlaine the Great.
Part the First*.   (Orig. 1590).   In *Elizabethan Tragedy*, ed. by George Rylands.   Bell,
1933.+

This is indicated by the reading notes (#16)
and is listed in Holleyman.

Specific quotes from (pp. 393-94):+

(a) I:i:[1-3]

(b) III:i:[50-53]; "withered" should read
"hindered"

(c) II:ii:[53-54]

(d) II:vii:[21-26]; "will" should read "wills"

(e) V:ii:[97-99, 106-10]

(14) Lady [Anne E.] Newdigate-Newdegate, *Gossip
from a Muniment Room* ...+   David Nutt, 1897.

This is indicated by the reading notes (B2c).

Last 3 quotes, p. 394, and first quote, p.
395, are from here.+

(15) William Shakespeare, *The Poems of ...*, ed.
by George Wyndham.+ Methuen, 1898.

This is indicated by the reading notes (B2c).

First quote, p. 396, is from here:

Rowland White to Sir Robert Sidney, Oct.
11, 1599

(16) "[Francis] Bacon in his Essays"

Bacon's Essays and Colours of Good and Evil,
ed. by W. Aldis Wright.+ Macmillan, 1862.
(Orig. 1597)

This is indicated by the reading notes (B2c).

(a) Specific quotes from:

    (i) 2nd quote, p. 396; 4th quote, p.
       397

       "Of Masques and Triumphs"; "be but"
       should read "are but."

    (ii) 3rd and 4th quotes, p. 396

       "Of Love"

    (iii) First quote, p. 397

       "Of Superstition"

    (iv) 2nd quote, p. 397

       "Of Praise"; there should be el-
       lipses after "naught."

    (v) 3rd quote, p. 397

       "Of Great Place"

(b) Essays named but not quoted from:

    "Of Truth"; "Of Death"; "Of Unity in Re-
    ligion"; "Of Revenge"; "Of Simulation
    and Dissimulation"

Important Allusion:

Geoffrey Chaucer, *The Canterbury Tales*. (Orig.
1387-94)

Passing Allusions:

(1) Miscellaneous writers:

    (a) Robert Browning, Raphael Holingshed,
Ben Jonson, Thomas Kyd, William Lang-
land, Alfred Lord Tennyson, John Wy-
cliffe

    (b) Mentioned by W. Harrison (see above):
Cicero, Pliny

(2) "the Pastons of Norfolk"

    Viz espec. the family letters, written be-
tween c.1420 and 1503, publ. orig. in 5
vols., 1787-89, 1823

    [Cf. "The Pastons and Chaucer," *Common Read-
er I.*]

(3) "the Betsons and Paycockes of Essex"

    E.g., see Eileen Power, *Medieval People*.+
Prob. ed.: Penguin Books, 1937. (Orig. 1924)

    This is listed in Holleyman Addendum.

(4) Works mentioned by Lady Clifford:

    (a) Philip Sidney, *The Arcadia*. (Orig.
1593)

    (b) Edmund Spenser, *The Faery Queen*. (See
above)

    (c) Michel Eyquem de Montaigne, *Essais*.
(Orig. 1580)

(5) Various plays by Shakespeare:

    (a) *Henry the Sixth*. (Orig. 1594)

    (b) *King John*. (Orig. publ. 1623)

    (c) *Hamlet*. (Orig. 1603)

    (d) *Antony and Cleopatra*. (Orig. publ. 1623)

    (e) *Macbeth*. (Orig. 1609)

    (f) *The Tempest*. (Orig. publ. 1623)

*   A PLUS SIGN (+), wherever it occurs, shows editor
Brenda Silver's hand in a bibliographical item.

APPRECIATIONS   C254
                                        Reading notes
    Obvious Source: B2o

        J[ohn] B[oynton] Priestley, *Figures in Modern
        Literature*. Lane, 1924.

    Important Allusions (mentioned by Priestley):

        Miscellaneous writers: Arnold Bennett, Maurice
        Hewlett, A[lfred] E[dward] Housman, W[illiam]
        W[ymark] Jacobs, Robert Lynd, George Saintsbury,
        George Santayana, J[ohn] C[ollings] Squire

    Passing Allusions (mentioned by Priestley):

        (1) Walter de la Mare, *The Veil*. (Orig. 1921)

        (2) Miscellaneous English writers: John Donne,
            William Hazlitt

- -

ARROWS OF FORTUNE (1905)   See p. 178, KP

    Obvious Source:

        Algernon Gissing, *Arrows of Fortune*. Bristol:
        Arrowsmith, 1905.

- -

ART AND LIFE (1909)   C34

    Obvious Source:

        Vernon Lee [pseud. of Violet Paget], *Laurus No-
        bilis*. Lane, 1909.

    Supportive Source:

        Plato, *The Symposium*. (Orig. c.368 B.C.) Poss.
        ed.: In Plato, *Dialogues*, trans. by B[enjamin]
        Jowett. 4 vol. Oxford: Clarendon, 1871. Vol. I.

        This is listed in Holleyman Addendum; it belonged
        to Leslie Stephen.

Passing Allusions (mentioned by Lee):

Miscellaneous English writers: Walter Pater,
John Ruskin

- -

ARTHUR YATES (1924)   C244.3

Obvious Source:

Arthur Yates and Bruce Blunt, *Arthur Yates: An
Autobiography*. Grant Richards, 1923.

- -

THE AUTHOR'S PROGRESS (1906)   C5.5
                                          Reading notes
Obvious Source: B1a

Adam Lorimer, *The Author's Progress*. Edinburgh:
Blackwood, 1906.

- -

BAD WRITERS (1918)   C132

Obvious Source:

Solomon Eagle [pseud. of J.C. Squire], *Books in
General*. Secker, 1918.

Specific quotes from:

(1) Cannot locate

(2) Florence Barclay, *The Wall of Partition*.
London and New York: G.P. Putnam's, 1914.

Important Allusion (mentioned by Eagle):

The New Statesman (periodical, 1913-31)

Passing Allusions:

> (1) Miscellaneous writers (mentioned by Eagle):
>
>> Matthew Arnold, Robert Bridges, Geoffrey Chaucer, Edward Gibbon, Henry James, John Keats, John Lyly, Walter Pater, William Shakespeare, Percy Bysshe Shelley, William Wordsworth
>
> (2) Various characters:
>
>> Falstaff; Mrs. Sarah Gamp (in Charles Dickens, *Martin Chuzzlewit* [1844])

- -

BARHAM OF BELTANA (1905)   C1.1
                                        Reading notes
    Obvious Source: B1a

> W[illiam] E[dward] Norris, *Barham of Beltana*. Methuen, 1905.

    Important Allusion:

> Anthony Trollope

- -

BEFORE THE MAST--AND AFTER (1924)   C250

    Obvious Source:

> Sir Walter Runciman, *Before the Mast--and After*. Fisher Unwin, 1924.

    Important Allusion:

> Joseph Conrad

BEHIND THE BRASS PLATE (1928)   C301.2

    Obvious Source:

        A.T. Schofield, *Behind the Brass Plate*. Sampson
        Low, 1928.

    Important Allusion (mentioned by Schofield):

        Thomas Carlyle

- -

BEHIND THE SCENES WITH CYRIL MAUDE (1928)   C301.1

    Obvious Source:

        [Cyril Maude], *Behind the Scenes* ... Murray,
        1928.

- -

A BELLE OF THE FIFTIES (1905)   C05
                                 Reading notes
    Obvious Source: B1a

        [Virginia Clay-Clopton], *A Belle of the Fifties:*
        Memoirs of Mrs. Clay, of Alabama, [ed.] by Ada
        Sterling. Heinemann, 1905.

    Important Allusion (mentioned by Clay-Clopton):

        Mrs. Malaprop (character in Richard Brinsley
        Sheridan, *The Rivals* [1775])

    Passing Allusions (mentioned by Clay-Clopton):

        (1) *Richmond Enquirer* (newspaper, 1844-77)

        (2) Aunt Ruthy Partington ("Yankee" character
            created by Benjamin P. Shillaber in series
            of comic works, 1847-90)

BLACKSTICK PAPERS (1908)   C20

Obvious Source:

Lady Anne Ritchie, *Blackstick Papers*.   Smith, Elder, 1908.

Specific essays quoted from:

(1) Quote 2

"Haydn"

(2) *Re* George Sand [pseud. of Amadine Aurora Lucie Dupin, Baroness Dudevant]

"Nohant in 1874"

(3) "Comparing modern women ... , she says"

"Links with the Past"

(4) "one passage"

Ibid.

Supportive Source:

"Sir Richard Jebb spoke once"; "to quote Sir Richard again"

Jebb to Caroline Lane Slemmer, Dec. 3, 1872

In *Life and Letters of Sir Richard Claverhouse Jebb*, ed. by Caroline Jebb.   Cambridge: Univ. Pr., 1907.

Passing Allusions (mentioned by Ritchie):

Miscellaneous writers: Ivan Tourgenieff, Horace Walpole

- -

BLANCHE ESMEAD (1906)   C3.7
                                         Reading notes
     Obvious Source: B1a

Mrs. [Ella] Fuller Maitland, *Blanche Esmead*. Methuen, 1906.

THE BLUEST OF THE BLUE (1906)   C5.3
                                       Reading notes
     Obvious Source: B1a

          Alice C.C. Gaussen, *A Woman of Wit and Wisdom*.
          Smith, Elder, 1906.

          Specific quote from:

          "[Samuel] Johnson ... wrote"

          To Elizabeth Carter, Jan. 14, 1756; repr. in
          Montagu Pennington, *Memoirs of ... Mrs. Eliza-
          beth Carter ...* (Orig. 1807)

     Important Allusion (mentioned by Gaussen):

          "her translation of Epictetus"

          Carter, trans.: Epictetus, *All the Works of ...*
          S. Richardson, A. Miller, 1758. (Orig. 1st
          cent. A.D.)

     Passing Allusion (mentioned by Gaussen):

          Elizabeth Montagu

- -

THE BOOK OF CATHERINE WELLS (1928)   C301.3

     Obvious Source:

          The Book of Catherine Wells, w/intro. by H.G.
          Wells. Chatto and Windus, 1928.

          Specific story mentioned:

          "The Emerald"

- -

A BOOK OF ESSAYS (1918)   C98

     Obvious Source:

          Robert Lynd, *If the Germans Conquered England*.
          Maunsel, 1917.

(1) Specific essay quoted from:

"Taking a Walk in London"

(2) Specific essays mentioned but not quoted
    from: "Horrors of War"; "Grub"; "Revenge";
    "Courage"; "Treating"; "Refugees"

Important Allusions:

(1) Charles Lamb, *The Essays of Elia*. (Orig.
    1823)

Specific essay mentioned:

"Mackery End"; orig. in *London Magazine*,
July 1821

(2) Michel Eyquem de Montaigne, *Essais*. (Orig.
    1580)

Passing Allusions:

(1) William Hazlitt

(2) William Makepeace Thackeray, *The Roundabout
    Papers*. (Orig. 1863)

- -

THE BROWN HOUSE AND CORDELIA (1905)   C2.12
                                         Reading notes
        Obvious Source: B1a

        Margaret Booth, *The Brown House and Cordelia*.
        Edward Arnold, 1905.

- -

BY BEACH AND BOGLAND (1905)   See p. 178, KP

        Obvious Source: Reading notes
                                         B1a
        Jane Barlow, *By Beach and Bogland*. T. Fisher
        Unwin, 1905.

BYRON AND MR. BRIGGS (1922; publ. in 1979)   C380; ed. by
                                             Edward A. Hun-
    Stated Impulse: gerford

        " ... 1922 was made memorable   Reading notes
        ... by a novel by E.K. Sanders   B2q
        called the Flame of Youth"

        The novelist (a.k.a. Ella Katha[e]rine Sandars
        by Library of Congress catalogue) existed but
        apparently not this title.

    Inferred Source:

        "Byron's letters"; "compositions by Shelley
        here ... placed beside them"

        *Lord Byron's Correspondence, Chiefly with Lady
        Melbourne, Mr. Hobhouse, the Hon. Douglas Kin-
        naird, and P.B. Shelley*, ed. by John Murray. 2
        vol. John Murray, 1922. Espec. Vol. II.

        This is listed in the reading notes.

        Specific letter mentioned:

        "Mary ... can hardly write for fury"

        Mary Shelley to Mrs. R.B. Hoppner, Aug. 11, 1821

    Supportive Sources:

        (1) *Re* William Shakespeare, *Measure for Measure*.
            (Orig. 1604)

            Samuel Taylor Coleridge, *The Lectures and
            Notes of 1818*. Poss. ed.: Coleridge, *Lec-
            tures and Notes on Shakspere and Other Eng-
            lish Poets*, coll. by T[homas] Ashe. Bohn's
            Standard Library ed. George Bell, 1885.
            (Orig. 1883)

            This is listed in Holleyman; it belonged to
            Leslie Stephen.

            Quote, pp. 329-30, is from here.

        (2) "Johnson ridiculed [Laurence Sterne's] Tris-
            tram Shandy"

            James Boswell, *The Life of Samuel Johnson,
            LL.D.* Poss. ed.: Ed. by James Birkbeck
            Hill. 6 vol. Oxford: Clarendon, 1887.
            (Orig. 1791) Vol. II.

(3) "Arnold thought [Percy Bysshe] Shelley's
    letters better than his poetry"

    Matthew Arnold, "Shelley"; orig. in *Nine-
    teenth Century*, Jan. 1888; repr. in Arnold,
    Essays in Criticism, Second Series. (Orig.
    1888) Prob. ed.: Macmillan, 1906.

    This is listed in Holleyman Addendum II.

(4) "Coleridge fell prostrate at the feet of
    Mr. [William L.] Bowles"

    In Coleridge, *Biographia Literaria.* (Orig.
    1817) Prob. ed.: Ed. by Henry Nelson Cole-
    ridge [and Sara Coleridge]. 2nd ed. 2 vol.
    William Pickering, 1847. Vol. I.

    This is listed in Holleyman; it belonged to
    Leslie Stephen.

(5) "Wordsworth thought" (p. 332)

    Paraphrase from William Wordsworth, "On the
    Extinction of the Venetian Republic." (Or-
    ig. 1807)

(6) "racing on the scent [of Lord Byron] with
    Lord Lovelace, and ... Mr Edgecumbe"

    (a) Ralphe Milbanke, Earl of Lovelace, *As-
        tarte.* Chiswick Pr., 1905.

        This is listed in Holleyman Addendum; it
        belonged to Thoby Stephen.

    (b) Richard Edgecumbe, *Byron: The Last Phase.*
        John Murray, 1909.

(7) Quatrain quoted on p. 337:

    16th-century lyric. Anonymous. In, e.g.,
    The English Poets, ed. by Thomas Humphry
    Ward. 4 vol. Oxford U. Pr., 1880-81. Vol.
    I.

(8) Geoffrey Chaucer, "Ballade de Bon Conseyl."
    (Orig. c.1389) In, e.g., *ibid.*

(9) Quotes, pp. 342-43:

    Poems by Robert Herrick

    (a) "Upon Prew His Maid"

    (b) "His Grange, or Private Wealth"

    (c) "An Epitaph Upon a Virgin"

(10) William Shakespeare, *Troilus and Cressida*. (Orig. 1609)

Quote, p. 346, is from here: I:iii:162-63.

(11) "Shakespeares [*sic*] daffodils"; should read "daffadils"

Shakespeare, *The Winter's Tale*: IV:iii:33; IV:iv:117. (Orig. publ. 1623)

(12) "the faery casements of Keats"; "faery" should read "magic" ("faery seas" occurs in the next line)

John Keats, "Ode to a Nightingale." (Orig. 1819)

Important Allusions:

(1) Joseph Conrad, *The Rescue*. Dent, 1920.

Woolf reviewed this for *TLS*, July 1, 1920, p. 419. (See "A Disillusioned Romantic.")

(2) "*The Vicar of Wakefield* has been reprinted again."

Oliver Goldsmith, *The Vicar of Wakefield*. (Orig. 1766)

(3) "getting at [Byron] through Leigh Hunt"

E.g., Hunt, *Autobiography*. (Orig. 1850)

(4) "getting at Leigh Hunt through his diary"

Cannot locate

(5) "getting at ... [Thomas] Moore through Mrs. [Bessy] Moore, and at Mrs Moore through Mrs Lynn Linton"

E.g., Mrs. [Eliza] Lynn Linton, *My Literary Life*. Hodder and Stoughton, 1899.

Passing Allusions:

(1) "Miss Sylvia Reddish issues her Thoughts at Dusk."

Imaginary author and attribution

(2) Miscellaneous literary critics: Joseph Addison, Aristotle, Nicolas Boileau, Denis Diderot, John Dryden, Anatole France, Rémy de Gourmont, Charles Augustin Sainte Beuve, Hippolyte-Adolphe Taine

(3) Shakespeare, *King Lear*. (Orig. publ. 1608)

(4) Miscellaneous British writers: Thomas Campion, Charles Darwin, Charles Dickens, George Eliot [pseud. of Mary Ann Evans], James Joyce, Andrew Marvell, W[illiam] E[dward] Norris, Algernon Charles Swinburne, H[erbert] G[eorge] Wells

(5) George Gordon, Lord Byron, *Don Juan*. (Orig. 1819-24)

(6) William Wordsworth, *The Prelude*. (Orig. 1850)

(7) Mentioned by Linton (see above): Walter Savage Landor

(8) Miscellaneous European writers: Dante Alighieri, Homer, Horace, Jean-Jacques Rousseau, Virgil

(9) Emily Brontë, *Wuthering Heights*. (Orig. 1847)

(10) Various Shakespeare characters: Othello, Hamlet, Falstaff

(11) Thomas Hardy, *Life's Little Ironies*. (Orig. 1894)

(12) Leo Tolstoy, *War and Peace*. (Orig. 1864-69)

- -

A CAMBRIDGE V.A.D. (1917)   C74

Obvious Source:

E.M. Spearing, *From Cambridge to Camiers Under the Red Cross*. Cambridge: Heffer, 1917.

THE CANDLE OF VISION (1918)   C129

    Obvious Source:

        A.E. [pseud. of George William Russell], *The
        Candle of Vision*. Macmillan, 1918.

    Important Allusions:

        (1) Thomas a Kempis

        (2) [Mariana Alcoforado?], *The Love Letters of a
            Portuguese Nun*. (Orig. in French 1669;
            first trans. in English 1702)

- -

CELEBRITIES OF OUR TIMES (1925)   C262.5

    Obvious Source:

        Herman Bernstein, *Celebrities of Our Times*.
        Hutchinson, 1925.

    Important Allusion (mentioned by Bernstein):

        George Bernard Shaw

    Passing Allusion (mentioned by Shaw):

        Leo Tolstoi, *What Is Art?* (Orig. 1898)

- -

THE "CENSORSHIP" OF BOOKS (1929)   C311

    Important Allusion:

        Aristotle

A CHARACTER SKETCH (1920)   C205

   Obvious Source:

> *Frederick Locker-Lampson*, composed and ed. by
> Augustine Birrell. Constable, 1920.
>
> Specific quote from:
>
> "what Mr. Hardy said"
>
> Thomas Hardy to Locker-Lampson, Feb. 2, 1880;
> (later repr. in Florence Emily Hardy, *The Early
> Life of Thomas Hardy, 1840-1891*. Macmillan,
> 1928)

   Important Allusion (mentioned by Birrell):

> William Makepeace Thackeray

   Passing Allusions:

> (1) Miscellaneous writers (mentioned by Birrell):
> Matthew Arnold, Robert Browning, George
> Eliot [pseud. of Mary Ann Evans], John Rus-
> kin, Francois Marie Arouet de Voltaire
>
> (2) Charles Lamb, *Essays of Elia*. (Orig. 1823)
>
> (3) Various traditional biographies:
>
>> (a) "the life of Thomas Henry Huxley in
>> two volumes"
>>
>> Leonard Huxley, *Life and Letters of Hux-
>> ley*. 2 vol. Macmillan, 1900.
>>
>> (b) "Alfred Tennyson by his son"
>>
>> Hallam Tennyson, *Alfred Lord Tennyson: A
>> Memoir*. (Orig. 1897)
>>
>> (c) "[Samuel Taylor] Coleridge by James Dyke
>> Campbell"
>>
>> Campbell, *Coleridge: A Narrative of the
>> Events of His Life*. (Orig. 1894)
>>
>> (d) "Samuel Barnett by his widow"
>>
>> Dame Henrietta Octavia Weston Barnett,
>> *Canon Barnett. His Life, Work and
>> Friends*. 2 vol. John Murray, 1918.

    (e) "Lord [Horatio Herbert] Kitchener by
        Sir George Arthur"

        Arthur, *Life of Lord Kitchener*. 3 vol.
        Macmillan, 1920.

    (f) "Lord Beaconsfield by Mr. Moneypenny
        [*sic*] and Mr. Buckle"

        William F. Monypenny and George Earle
        Buckle, *The Life of* [Benjamin] *Disraeli*.
        6 vol. John Murray, 1910-20.

- -

CHARLOTTE BRONTË (1916)*   C52

    Supportive Sources:

        Novels by Brontë:

        (1) *Jane Eyre*. (Orig. 1847)

            First quote is from here.

        (2) *Villette*. (Orig. 1853)

            All quotes, paragraph 7, are from here.

    Important Allusion:

        "Mrs. Gaskell stamped our minds"

        I.e., Elizabeth Gaskell, *The Life of Charlotte
        Brontë*. (Orig. 1857) Prob. ed.: Smith, Elder,
        1865.

        This is listed in Holleyman; it belonged to Les-
        lie Stephen.

    Passing Allusions:

        (1) William Shakespeare, *Hamlet*. (Orig. 1603)

        (2) Fyodor Dostoevsky, *The Idiot*. (Orig. 1882)

        (3) Thomas Hardy, *Jude the Obscure*. (Orig. 1895)

        (4) Leo Tolstoy

*   This essay contributed to "'Jane Eyre' and 'Wuthering
Heights'" in *Common Reader I*.

CHARLOTTE BRONTË (1917) C93

Obvious Source:

> *Charlotte Brontë ... : A Centenary Memorial*, ed.
> by Butler Wood. Fisher Unwin, 1917.

> Specific essays quoted from:

> (1) "The essay by Mrs. [Mary Augusta] Humphry Ward"

> "Some Thoughts on Charlotte Brontë"; first quote should begin with "shaping"

> (2) "Mr. Gosse interrupts"

> Edmund Gosse, "A Word on Charlotte Brontë"

> (3) "cut short by Bishop [J.E.C.] Welldon"

> "Centenary Address at Haworth"

> (4) "Dr. [Richard] Garnett tells us"

> "The Place of Charlotte Brontë in Nineteenth Century Fiction"

> (5) "reversed ... by Professor [C.E.] Vaughan"

> "Charlotte and Emily Brontë"

> (6) "one critic, Mr. [G.K.] Chesterton"

> "Charlotte Brontë as a Romantic"

Important Allusion:

> "'in [Charlotte's] own words'" (quoted by Gosse)

> Cannot locate

Passing Allusions:

> (1) Mentioned by Ward:

>> (a) Ernest Renan

>> (b) Charlotte Brontë, *Shirley*. (Orig. 1849)

> (2) Mentioned by Gosse: Honoré de Balzac

> (3) Mentioned by Vaughan: Leo Tolstoy

CHATEAU AND COUNTRY LIFE (1908)   C18

    Obvious Source:

        Mary King Waddington, *Chateau and Country Life in France.* Smith, Elder, 1908.

    Passing Allusion (mentioned by Waddington):

        Jean Baptiste Poquelin Molière

- -

THE CHERRY ORCHARD (1920)   C201

    Supportive Source:

        Anton Tchekhov, *The Cherry Orchard.* (Orig. 1903-04)

    Important Allusion:

        Richard Brinsley Sheridan, *The School for Scandal.* (Orig. 1781)

    Passing Allusion:

        Oscar Wilde

- -

THE CHINESE SHOE (1923)   C240.1

    Obvious Source:

        Kathleen Fitzpatrick, *Lady Henry Somerset.* Cape, 1923.

    Passing Allusion (mentioned by Fitzpatrick):

        Alfred Lord Tennyson

CHINESE STORIES (1913)   C49.1

Obvious Source:

P'ou Song-lin, *Strange Stories from the Lodge of Leisure*, trans. by George Soulié de Morant. Constable, 1913. (Orig. 18th cent.)

(1) Specific stories quoted from:

(a) "one of the stories begins"

"Through Many Lives"

(b) "Take, for example, the following"

"The Ghost in Love"

(2) Stories mentioned but not quoted from:

(a) "The Spirit of the River"

(b) "The River of Sorrows"

Passing Allusions:

(1) Mentioned by Soulié:

Chen Shou, *History of the Three Kingdoms*. (Orig. 3rd cent. A.D.)

(2) Miscellaneous English novelists: Henry Fielding, Samuel Richardson

- -

CLARA BUTT: HER LIFE STORY (1928)   C301.5

Obvious Source:

Winifred Ponder, *Clara Butt: Her Life Story*. Harrap, 1928.

Passing Allusion (mentioned by Ponder):

"Abide with Me": traditional hymn with words by Henry Francis Lyte (1847?); music, "Eventide," by William H. Monk (1861)

THE COMPROMISE (1906)   C5.1

    Obvious Source: Reading notes
                                                B1a
        Dorothea Gerard, *The Compromise*. Hutchinson,
        1906.

- -

CONGREVE (1921)   C217

    Supportive Source:

        William Congreve, *Love for Love*. Poss. ed.:
        The Dramatic Works of Wycherley, Congreve, Van-
        brugh, and Farquhar, ed. by Leigh Hunt. G.
        Routledge, 1883. (Orig. 1840; play orig. 1695)

        This is listed in Holleyman; it belonged to Leo-
        nard.

        Specific quotes from:

        (1) First paragraph

            (a) I:[xiii]:500-02

            (b) V:[x]:370-71

        (2) Fourth paragraph

            IV:[xx]:679-83; "our" should be in brackets

    Passing Allusions:

        Miscellaneous English novelists: George Mere-
        dith, Thomas Love Peacock

- -

CONGREVE (1925)   C268.1

    Obvious Source: Reading notes
                                                  #18
        William Congreve, *Comedies by* ..., ed. by Bon-
        amy Dobrée. Oxford U. Pr., 1925.

        Specific play mentioned: *The Way of the World*.
        (Orig. 1700)

Important Allusion:

"a second volume [to come]"

I.e., Congreve, *The Mourning Bride, Poems, and Miscellanies*, ed. by Dobrée. World's Classics ser. Oxford U. Pr., 1928.

Passing Allusions:

(1) Miscellaneous English playwrights: George Farquhar, William Shakespeare, Sir John Vanbrugh, William Wycherley

(2) Congreve, *The Mourning Bride*. (Orig. 1697)

(3) "Nonesuch Press edition"

   The Complete Works of William Congreve, ed. by Montague Summers. 4 vol. Nonesuch Pr., 1923.

(4) Lady Wishfort (character in *The Way of the World*)

- -

CONISTON (1906)   C5.4

   Obvious Source: Reading notes
                                      B1a
         Winston Churchill [American], *Coniston*. Macmillan, 1906.

- -

A COOKERY BOOK (1909)   C38

   Obvious Source:

         The Cookery Book of Lady Clark of Tillypronte, arr. and ed. by Catherine Frances Frere. Constable, 1909.

         Specific quote from:

         François Marie Arouet de Voltaire [on digestion]

         Cannot locate

Passing Allusion (mentioned by Lady Clark):

"the poet Rogers"

Samuel Rogers

- -

LES COPAINS (1913)   C49.3

Obvious Source:

Jules Romains, *Les Copains*. Paris: Eugene Figuière, 1913.

Important Allusions:

(1) Jules Romains, *Mort de Quelqu'un*. Paris:
Eugene Figuière, 1911.

(2) Miscellaneous writers: G[ilbert] K[eith]
Chesterton, François Rabelais.

- -

THE CORNISH MINER (1928)   C297.2

Obvious Source:

A.K. Hamilton Jenkin(s), *The Cornish Miner*. Allen and Unwin, 1927.

- -

CREATIVE CRITICISM (1917)   C77

Obvious Source:

J[oel] E[lias] Spingarn, *Creative Criticism*.
New York: Holt, 1917.

Specific quote from:

"it is possible to say"

Ralph Waldo Emerson, "The Rhodora." (Orig.
1839)

Supportive Source:

> "Dr. Johnson ... asked"

> Paraphrase from Samuel Johnson, *Rasselas*. (Orig. 1759) Poss. ed.: In Johnson, *Works...* , ed. by Arthur Murphy. 12 vol. (Orig. in this ed. 1792) Vol. III.

> Two sets are listed in Holleyman:

> (1) 1806

>> This belonged to Leslie Stephen.

> (2) 1810

> Both were published by T. Longman.

Passing Allusions:

> (1) Miscellaneous literary critics (mentioned by Spingarn): Thomas Carlyle, Horace, Charles Augustin Sainte Beuve

> (2) Works by Samuel Taylor Coleridge:

>> (a) *Notes and Lectures upon Shakespeare*. (Orig. publ. 1849)

>> (b) *The Rime of the Ancient Mariner*. (Orig. 1798)

- -

A DARK LANTERN (1905)   C1.3

> Obvious Source: Reading notes
>   B1a
>> Elizabeth Robins, *A Dark Lantern*. Heinemann, 1905.

DAY IN, DAY OUT (1928)   C301.6

    Obvious Source:

        Aubrey [i.e., Elizabeth Alice Frances] Le
        Blond, *Day In, Day Out.* Bodley Head, 1928.

    Important Allusion (mentioned by Le Blond):

        "[her] well-known book on Italian gardens"

        The Old Gardens of Italy, How to Visit Them.
        (Orig. 1912; 2nd ed., rev., 1926)

- -

THE DAYS OF DICKENS (1926)   C272.3

    Obvious Source:

        Arthur L. Hayward, *The Days of* [Charles] *Dickens.*
        Routledge, [1926].

    Passing Allusion (mentioned by Hayward):

        William Makepeace Thackeray

- -

DAYS THAT ARE GONE (1924)   C249.1

    Obvious Source:

        B[ulmer] de Sales la Terrière, *Days that Are Gone.*
        Hutchinson, 1924.

    Specific quote from:

    Re "great wits":

        John Dryden, "Absalom and Achitophel." (Orig.
        1680) Part I, line 63.

    Important Allusion (mentioned by la Terrière):

        Oscar Wilde

THE DEBTOR (1905)   C2.8

    Obvious Source: Reading notes
                                           B1a
        Mary E. Wilkins [Freeman], *The Debtor*. Harper,
        1905.

    Passing Allusion:

        Elizabeth Gaskell, *Cranford*. (Orig. 1853)

- -

THE DECAY OF ESSAY-WRITING (1905)   C07

    Important Allusions:

        (1) Michel Eyquem de Montaigne

        (2) By Charles Lamb:

            (a) *Essays of Elia*. (Orig. 1823)

            (b) Second ser. (Orig. 1828)

            (c) *Last Essays of Elia*. (Orig. 1833)

    Passing Allusions:

        Miscellaneous classical writers: Aeschylus,
        Homer

- -

"DELTA" (1905)   C2.13

    Obvious Source: Reading notes
                                           B1a
        D[avid] M[acbeth] Moir, *The Life of Mansie Wauch,
        Taylor in Dalkeith*, ed. [w/memoir] by Thomas
        Aird. New ed. Edinburgh: Blackwood, 1905.
        (Orig. 1828)   ["Delta" was Moir's pseudonym.]

        Specific quotes from (quoted by Aird):

        (1) "His brother [Charles] ... tells us"

            Narrative in MS

(2) "Jeffrey wrote"

    Re "one of Moir's poems" [*sic*; i.e., collection of poems]

    Sir Francis Jeffrey to Moir, n.d. given

(3) "[Thomas] Carlyle exclaimed"

    Cannot locate

Passing Allusions (mentioned by Aird):

(1) Horace

(2) *Blackwood's Magazine* (periodical, 1817-present)

- -

A DESCRIPTION OF THE DESERT (1905)   C2.11

  Obvious Source: Reading notes
                                        B1a
    Gilbert Watson, *The Voice of the South*. Hurst and Blackett, 1905.

  Supportive Source:

    "wrote Kinglake"

    Alexander William Kinglake, *Eothen*. (Orig. 1844)

    3 poss. editions:

    (1) Travellers Library ed. 1851.

    (2) New ed. N.p., 1859.

    (3) New ed. N.p., 1864.

    All are listed in Holleyman; they belonged to George Duckworth, Laura Stephen, and Herbert Duckworth respectively.

THE DEVIL'S DUE (1905)   C2.6

    Obvious Source: Reading notes
                                           B1a
        G.B. Burgin, *The Devil's Due*. Hutchinson,
        1905.

- -

THE DIARIES OF MARY, COUNTESS OF MEATH (1928)   C303.1

    Obvious Source:

        The Diaries of Mary, Countess of Meath, ed. by
        her husband [Reginald Brabazon]. Hutchinson,
        1928. [Vol. I of 2.]

    Passing Allusion (mentioned by Lady Mary):

        Bertrand Russell

- -

DICKENS BY A DISCIPLE (1919)   C145

    Obvious Source:

        W. Walter Crotch, *The Secret of Dickens*. Chap-
        man and Hall, 1919.

    Important Allusions (mentioned by Crotch):

        (1) Miscellaneous writers: Nathaniel Hawthorne,
            Sir Walter Scott, William Shakespeare

        (2) Various works:

            (a) Charles Dickens, *Nicholas Nickleby*.
                (Orig. 1839)

            (b) By William Makepeace Thackeray:

                (i) *Vanity Fair*.   (Orig. 1848)

                (ii) *Henry Esmond*.   (Orig. 1852)

    Passing Allusions:

        (1) Miscellaneous novelists:

       (a) Edna Lyall [pseud. of Ada Edna Bayly]

       (b) Mentioned by Crotch: Willkie Collins,
           Henry Fielding, Elizabeth Gaskell, Bret
           Harte, Charles Kingsley, Rudyard Kip-
           ling, Charles Reade, Samuel Richardson

    (2) King Lear

- -

A DISILLUSIONED ROMANTIC (1920)   C197

    Obvious Source:

        Joseph Conrad, *The Rescue.*   Dent, 1920.

    Supportive Sources:

        Novels by Conrad:

        (1) *Chance.* (Orig. 1913)

           Poss. ed.: Methuen, 1914.

           This is listed in Holleyman.

        (2) *Victory.*

           Poss. ed.: Methuen, 1915.

- -

DREAMS AND REALITIES (1918)   C110

    Obvious Source:

        Walter de la Mare, *Motley and Other Poems.* Con-
        stable, 1918.

        (1) Specific poems quoted from:

           (a) Paragraph 2:

               (i) "The Three Strangers"

               (ii) "The Sunken Garden"

               (iii) "The Empty House"; "Wail" should
                     read "Wails"

        (b) Paragraph 3:

                (i) Quotes 1-3

                   "Vain Questioning"

                (ii) "Life"; there should be ellipses before "empty"

                (iii) "Fare Well"

    (2) Poems mentioned but not quoted from:

        (a) "Happy England"

        (b) "E.T."

        (c) "Eyes"

Passing Allusion:

    William Wordsworth, *The Prelude.* (Orig. 1850)

- -

THE DUKE AND DUCHESS OF NEWCASTLE-UPON-TYNE (1911)   C46

    Obvious Source:

        [Thomas Longueville], *The Duke and Duchess of Newcastle-upon-Tyne.* Longmans, 1910.

        Specific quotes from:

        (1) Paragraph 2:

            (a) "writes the Duchess"

                Margaret Cavendish, *The Life of William Cavendish.* (See below)

            (b) "the editor exclaims"

                I.e., Longueville, whose name does not occur on the title page

        (2) Paragraph 3:

            (a) From Clarendon (see below); Woolf added "and art"

(b) Margaret Cavendish, *Natures Pictures Drawn by Fancies Pencil* ... J. Martin and J. Allestrye, 1656.

(c) Anon., *Biographia Britannica*. (Orig. 1747)

(d) Edward Hyde, Earl of Clarendon, *The History of the Rebellion* ... (Orig. 1719)

(e) *Re* William Davenant:

Sir Philip Warwick, *Memoirs of the Reigne of King Charles I*. (Orig. 1701)

Last quote, paragraph 3, is also from here (quoted by M. Cavendish, *The Life of William Cavendish* [see below])

(f) "he declared"

William Cavendish to Prince Rupert (Count Palatine), June/July, 1644

Apparently oral tradition

(3) Paragraph 4:

(a) "as [the Duchess] has it"

Cannot locate

(b) "They called her"

Emile Montegut, *Le Duc et la Duchesse de Newcastle*. Paris: N.p., 1895.

There should be ellipses after "fool" and "Madge."

(c) "Mr. Pepys"

Samuel Pepys, *Diary*. (Orig. 1825) May 1, 1667.

(d) "said Count [Philibert de] Grammont"

[Anthony Hamilton], *Memoirs of ... Count Grammont*. (Orig. 1713)

(4) Paragraph 5:

(a) First quote

In M. Cavendish, *CCXI Sociable Letters*. (See below)

Should read: " ... those women are best bred, whose minds are civilest."

(b) Quotes 2 and 4

Cannot locate

(c) *Re* "fools"

"Of a Fool"; "your" should be in brackets

In M. Cavendish, *Poems and Fancies*. J. Martyn and J. Allestrye, 1653.

Supportive Sources:

(1) "writes the Duchess" (paragraph 2)

Margaret Cavendish, Duchess of Newcastle, *The Life of William Cavendish, Duke of Newcastle*. (Orig. 1667) Prob. ed.: Ed. by C. H. Firth. 2nd ed., rev. G. Routledge, [1906].

This is listed in Holleyman; it belonged to Virginia.

(2) "the Duke remarked"

His preface to M. Newcastle, *Philosophical and Physical Opinions*. J. Martin and J. Allestrye, 1655.

(3) Horace Walpole, *A Catalogue of the Royal and Noble Authors of England*. (Orig. 1758)

The episode about "John" [Rolleston], paragraph 4, is from here.

(4) "she declared" (quote 3, paragraph 5); "rashly" should read "hastily," and "there" should be in brackets

M. Cavendish, *CCXI Sociable Letters*. William Wilson, 1664.

Quote 5, paragraph 5, is also from here.

Important Allusions:

(1) Mentioned by Longueville: "his great work"

William Cavendish, *A New Method and Extraordinary Invention to Dress Horses*. (Orig. 1667)

(2) Mentioned by Lady Margaret: Thomas Hobbes

Passing Allusions:

(1) Miscellaneous writers:

   (a) Mentioned by Longueville: Ben Jonson, Sir John Suckling, Sir Henry Wotton

   (b) Mentioned by Lady Margaret: René Descartes

   (c) Sir Thomas Browne

(2) "[Charles] Lamb's praises [of Lady Margaret]":

   (a) Mentioned by Longueville (see above):

      (i) "The Two Races of Men," orig. in *London Magazine*, Dec. 1820; repr. in Lamb, *Essays of Elia*. (Orig. 1823)

      (ii) "Mackery End," orig. in *London Magazine*, July 1821; repr. in *Essays of Elia*.

   (b) "A Complaint of the Decay of Beggars in the Metropolis," orig. in *London Magazine*, June 1822; repr. in *Essays of Elia*.

   (c) "Detached Thoughts on Books and Reading," orig. in *London Magazine*, July 1822; repr. in *Last Essays of Elia*. (Orig. 1833)

- -

EDITIONS-DE-LUXE (1924)   C253

Obvious Sources:

   (1) William Shakespeare, *A Midsummer Night's Dreame*, w/intro. by Harley Granville-Barker. E. Benn, 1924. (Orig. publ. 1623)

   (2) Clifford Bax, *Studio Plays: Three Experiments in Dramatic Form*. Palmer, 1924.

THE ENGLISH MAIL COACH (1906)

See p. 179, #7, KP

Obvious Source:

Reading notes
B1a

Thomas De Quincey, "The English Mail-Coach"; orig. in *Blackwood's Magazine*, 1849. Prob. ed.: In *De Quincey's Writings*. (See below.)

(Woolf mentions "The writings [of De Quincey]... that formidable row....")

Supportive Sources:

Other works by De Quincey:

(1) "the *Autobiography*"

Autobiographic Sketches; orig., as "Sketches of Men and Manners from the Autobiography of an English Opium Eater," in *Tait's Edinburgh Magazine*, 1834-40, *passim*. In *De Quincey's Writings. Selections Grave and Gay*. 14 vol. Edinburgh: James Hogg, 1853-60. Vol. I [of 2].

This is indicated by the reading notes.

First quote, paragraph 3, is from here.

(2) First quote, paragraph 4

Cannot locate

(3) *Suspiria de Profundis*; orig. in *Blackwood's Magazine*, 1845. Prob. ed.: In *De Quincey's Writings*. (See above.)

Last 2 quotes, paragraph 4, are from here.

Important Allusions:

(1) De Quincey, "the *Lake Poets*"

Recollections of the Lakes and the Lake Poets; orig. in *Tait's Edinburgh Magazine*, 1839-40, *passim*.

(2) Robert Louis Stevenson

Passing Allusion:

Walter Pater

THE ESSAYS OF AUGUSTINE BIRRELL (1930)   C323

>   Inferred Source (stated in first   Reading notes
>   paragraph):   #s13 and 20
>   "a [new] book by Mr. Birrell"
>
>   Augustine Birrell, *Et Cetera*. Chatto and Win-
>   dus, 1930.
>
>   Specific quote from:
>
>   P. 37, quote 2
>
>   "Nathaniel Hawthorne." (Orig. 1928)
>
>   Supportive Source:
>
>   Augustine Birrell, *The Collected Essays and Ad-
>   dresses of* ...   3 vol.   J.M. Dent, 1922.
>
>   This is listed in the reading notes (#13) and
>   in Holleyman; it belonged to Virginia.
>
>   Specific quotes from:
>
>   (1) Pp. 30-31
>
>   "Preface"
>
>   (2) P. 33
>
>   "The House of Commons." (Orig. 1896) In
>   Vol. III.
>
>   There should be ellipses between "your" and
>   "constituencies."
>
>   (3) P. 34
>
>   Quotes 1-2:
>
>   "The Muse of History." (Orig. 1887) In
>   Vol. III.
>
>   (4) P. 35
>
>   "Truth-Hunting." (Orig. 1884) In Vol. III.
>
>   (5) P. 36
>
>   (a) "John Wesley." (Orig. 1902) In Vol. I.
>
>   (b) "Matthew Arnold." (Orig. 1892) In Vol.
>   II.

(6) P. 37

    First quote:

    "Dr. Johnson." (Orig. 1887) In Vol. I.

(7) P. 38

    "Charles Lamb." (Orig. 1887) In Vol. II.

    There should be ellipses before "read."

Important Allusions:

    (1) Other works by Birrell:

        (a) *Obiter Dicta*. (Orig. 1884, 1887)

        (b) *Res Judicatae*. (Orig. 1892)

        (c) *Essays About Men, Women and Books*. (Orig. 1894)

    (2) "Thackeray's judgment upon [Laurence] Sterne"

        William Makepeace Thackeray, *The English Humourists*. (Orig. 1853)

    (3) "Carlyle's judgment upon [Charles] Lamb"

        Thomas Carlyle, *Reminiscences*, ed. by James Anthony Froude. (Orig. 1881)

    (4) "Arnold's judgment on [Percy Bysshe] Shelley"

        Matthew Arnold, "Shelley," *Essays in Criticism. Second Series*. (Orig. 1888)

Passing Allusions:

    (1) Miscellaneous British writers (mentioned by Birrell): George Borrow, Robert Browning, Samuel Taylor Coleridge, Charles Dickens, George Eliot [pseud. of Mary Ann Evans], W[illiam] E[rnest] Henley, Samuel Johnson, Hannah More, Sir Walter Scott

    (2) Quoted by Birrell:

        William Shakespeare, *Hamlet*, III:i:85. (Orig. 1603)

    (3) Various works:

    (a) Mentioned by Birrell:

        (i) Robert Louis Stevenson, *Treasure Island*. (Orig. 1883)

        (ii) Nathaniel Hawthorne, *A Wonder Book*. (Orig. 1852)

    (b) Not mentioned by Birrell:

        (i) Marcel Proust, *A la Recherche du Temps Perdu*. (Orig. 1914-27)

        (ii) George Meredith, *The Egoist*. (Orig. 1879)

        (iii) Henry James, *The Wings of the Dove*. (Orig. 1902)

        (iv) Thomas Hardy, *The Return of the Native*. (Orig. 1878)

        (v) Fyodor Dostoevsky, *The Possessed*. (Orig. 1873)

        (vi) Joseph Conrad, *Lord Jim*. (Orig. 1900)

- -

ETHEL SMYTH (1921)   C218

    Obvious Source:

        Ethel Smyth, *Streaks of Life*. Longmans, Green, 1921.

    Important Allusion:

        Ethel Smyth, *Impressions That Remained*. 2 vol. Longmans, Green, 1919.

THE FACE OF CLAY (1906)   C3.8

    Obvious Source: Reading notes
                                           B1a
        H[orace] A[nnesley] Vachell, *The Face of Clay*.
        Murray, 1906.

- -

FANTASY (1921)   C224

    Obvious Source:

        L[awrence] P[earsall] Jacks, *Legends of Smoke-
        over*. Hodder and Stoughton, 1921.

    Supportive Source:

        François Marie Arouet de Voltaire, *Candide*.
        (Orig. 1759)

        3 poss. eds. listed in Holleyman:

        (1) *Oeuvres. Complètes*...   70 vol. Paris:
            L'Imprimerie de la Société Littéraire-
            Typographique, 1784-89. Vol. XLIV.

            This belonged to Leonard.

        (2) *Romans de Voltaire*. [3 vol.] Paris: Pierre
            Didot, 1800. Vol. I [only].

            This belonged to Leslie Stephen.

        (3) *Romans de Voltaire. Suivis des Ses Contes* ...
            Paris: Garnier, n.d.

            This belonged to Leslie Stephen.

        Last quote in essay is from here.

    Passing Allusions:

        Miscellaneous English novelists: Samuel Butler,
        E[dward] M[organ] Forster, Felicia Hemans, Thom-
        as Love Peacock

THE FEMININE NOTE IN FICTION (1905)   See p. 178, KP

    Obvious Source:

        W[illiam] L[eonard] Courtney, *The Feminine Note in Fiction*. Chapman and Hall, 1904.

    Passing Allusions:

    Miscellaneous women writers:

        (1) Mentioned by Courtney: Jane Austen, Mrs. Humphry Ward (b. Mary Augusta Arnold)

        (2) Sappho

- -

THE FIGHTING NINETIES (1916)   C55.1

    Obvious Source:

        Elizabeth Robins Pennell, *Nights*. Heinemann, 1916.

    Passing Allusions:

    Miscellaneous English writers:

        (1) Matthew Arnold

        (2) Mentioned by Pennell: Henry Harland, W[illiam] E[rnest] Henley

- -

A FLOOD TIDE (1905)   C2.9

    Obvious Source: Reading notes
                                   B1a
        Mary Debenham, *A Flood Tide*. Edward Arnold, 1905.

THE FLURRIED YEARS (1926)   C272.4

  Obvious Source:

    [Isobel] Violet Hunt, *The Flurried Years*.
    Hurst and Blackett, [1926].

  Important Allusion (mentioned by Hunt):

    Henry James

  Passing Allusions (mentioned by Hunt):

    (1) Miscellaneous writers: Joseph Conrad,
        W[illiam] H[enry] Hudson

    (2) Miss Flite (character in Charles Dickens,
        Bleak House [1853])

- -

A FLYING LESSON (1920)   C212

  Obvious Source:

    Max Beerbohm, *And Even Now*. Heinemann, 1920.

  Important Allusions:

    (1) Miscellaneous English essayists: Joseph
        Addison, William Hazlitt, Charles Lamb

    (2) Mentioned by Beerbohm: Algernon Charles
        Swinburne

- -

FORGOTTEN BENEFACTORS (1919)   C157

  Obvious Source:

    *Edward Jerningham and His Friends: A Series of
    Eighteenth-Century Letters*, ed. by Lewis Bet-
    tany. Chatto and Windus, 1919.

    Specific quotes from:

    (1) "A friend remarked"

[Thomas James Mathias], *The Pursuits of Literature.* 4 "Parts." J. Owen, 1794-97.

(2) "an anecdote told by his niece"

Charlotte Jerningham, diary, Aug. 12, 1809

(3) "another extract"

Ibid., July 27, 1809

(4) "she concludes an account"

Ibid.

(5) *Re* "la Belle Emilie['s] ... fair friend"

Elizabeth, Countess of Harcourt, to Jerningham, Aug. 29, [1790?]

(6) "writes Lady Harcourt"

Ibid.

(7) "on another occasion"

M.D. Harland to Jerningham, Dec. 21, 1782

(8) *Re* Lord Harcourt's death (quoted by Bettany)

The Annual Register ... for the Year 1777. J. Dodsley, 1778.

(9) "Lord Harcourt ... wrote"

Simon, Earl of Harcourt, to Jerningham, March 29, 1773

(10) "[Lady Mount Edgecumbe] was known"

Lady Sarah Fane Jersey to Jerningham, Aug. 5, 1791

(11) "Lady Mount Edgecumbe['s] ... style"

Emma, Countess of Mount Edgecumbe, to Jerningham, July 9, 1794

(12) *Re* "war with France"

Same to same, Sept. 20, [1794]

Passing Allusion (mentioned by Jerningham):

Thomas Gray

THE FORTUNES OF FARTHINGS (1905)   C1.2

    Obvious Source: Reading notes
                                        B1a
        A.J. Dawson, *The Fortunes of Farthings*. Harper, 1905.

- -

FRANCES WILLARD (1912)   C49

    Obvious Source:

        Ray Strachey, *Frances Willard. Her Life and Work*. Fisher Unwin, 1912.

- -

FRAULEIN SCHMIDT AND MR. ANSTRUTHER (1907) C5.10

    Obvious Source:

        Elizabeth [pseud. of Elizabeth Mary von Arnim, later Countess Russell], *Fraulein Schmidt and Mr. Anstruther*. Smith, Elder, 1907.

    Supportive Source (paraphrased by Elizabeth):

        Christina Rossetti, "Song" ["When I am dead, my dearest"]. (Orig. 1848) Prob. ed.: C. Rossetti, *Poetical Works*, w/notes and memoir by William Michael Rossetti. Macmillan, 1906.

        This is listed in Holleyman Addendum.

        Last quote in essay is from here.

    Passing Allusions (mentioned by Elizabeth):

        Miscellaneous writers: Johann Wolfgang von Goethe, Friedrich Schiller, Robert Louis Stevenson, Walt Whitman

FROM HALL-BOY TO HOUSE-STEWARD (1925)   C269.4

Obvious Source:

W[illiam] Lanceley, *From Hall-Boy to House-Steward*. Arnold, 1925.

Passing Allusion (mentioned by Lanceley):

Oscar Wilde

- -

FURTHER REMINISCENCES (1925)   C261.1

Obvious Source:

S[abine] Baring-Gould, *Further Reminiscences, 1864-1894*. Bodley Head, 1925.

Specific quotes from [letters]:

(1) Baring-Gould to Rev. J. M. Gatrill, March 13, 1889

(2) *Ibid.*

(3) Same to same, Feb. 28, 1889

- -

GENTLEMEN ERRANT (1909)   C32

Obvious Source:

Mrs. [Emmeline] Henry Cust, *Gentlemen Errant*. John Murray, 1909.

Important Allusions (mentioned by Cust):

Miscellaneous German writers: Albrecht von Eyb, Hans von Schweinichen [und Mertschuetz]

Passing Allusions:

(1) Edmund Spenser, *The Faerie Queen*. (Orig. 1590, 1596)

(2) Miscellaneous English writers: Daniel Defoe, William Shakespeare

GEORGE ELIOT (1926)   C276.2

Obvious Source:

George Eliot, *The Letters of* ..., selected by
R. Brimley Johnson. Bodley Head, 1926.

Specific quotes from:

(1) Paragraph 2:

Mary Ann Evans [later George Eliot] to Ma-
ria Lewis, June 23, 1840

(2) Paragraph 3:

(a) "Mr. Bray said"

Charles Bray, *Phases of Opinion and Ex-
perience During a Long Life*. (Orig.
1884)

(b) George Eliot to Edward Burne-Jones,
March 20, 1873

Quote should start with "historical";
there should be ellipses after "of"

(c) Same to Sara Hennell, Dec. 7, 1866

(d) Same to same, Apr. 16, 1857

Important Allusion:

"Mr. Cross ... pruned the letters"

*George Eliot's Life as Related in Her Letters
and Journals*, arr. and ed. by J.W. Cross. (Orig.
1884)

Passing Allusions (mentioned by Eliot):

(1) "Hannah More's letters"

E.g., W. Roberts, *Memoirs of the Life and
Correspondence of Mrs. Hannah More*. (Orig.
1834)

(2) "Doddridge's Sermons"

In Philip Doddridge, *Works*. 10 vol. Leeds:
n.p., 1802.

(3) Miscellaneous writers: George Henry Lewes,
Sophocles

GEORGIANA AND FLORENCE (1940)   C371

    Obvious Source:

        Georgiana Swinton [and Florence Sitwell], *Two Generations*, ed. by Osbert Sitwell. Macmillan, 1940.

    Passing Allusions:

        (1) Mentioned by Georgiana:

            (a) "the memoirs of Napoleon"

                Louis Antoine Fauvelet de Bourrienne, *Mémoire de M. de B* [*sic*], ... *sur Napoléon*... (Orig. 1829)

            (b) "the *Histoire de Venice*"

                Probably: Pierre Daru, *Histoire de la République de Venise.* (Orig. 1819)

        (2) Mentioned by Florence: Charles Darwin

- -

GIPSY OR GOVERNESS? (1925)   C262.4

    Obvious Source:

        Margot Asquith, *Places and Persons.* Thornton Butterworth, 1925.

    Passing Allusions:

        (1) Miscellaneous writers:

            (a) Lady Hester Stanhope

            (b) Mentioned by Asquith: Plato, John Addington Symonds, Alfred Lord Tennyson, Oscar Wilde

        (2) Mentioned by Asquith:

            A[rthur] S[tuart] M[enteth] Hutchinson, *If Winter Comes.* (Orig. 1921)

THE GLEN O' WEEPING (1907)   C5.11

Obvious Source:

Marjorie Bowen, *The Glen o' Weeping*. Alston
Rivers, 1907.

Passing Allusions (mentioned by Bowen):

Miscellaneous British writers: David Hume, Tobias Smollett

- -

GLIMPSES OF AUTHORS (1924)   C244.1

Obvious Source:

Caroline Ticknor, *Glimpses of Authors*. Werner
Laurie, 1923.

Important Allusions (mentioned by Ticknor):

Miscellaneous English novelists: Jane Austen,
Charles Dickens

Passing Allusions (mentioned by Ticknor):

Miscellaneous English writers: Samuel Taylor
Coleridge, Lady Anne Ritchie

- -

A GOOD DAUGHTER (1920)   C192.1

Obvious Source:

Constance Hill, *Mary Russell Mitford and Her Surroundings*. Lane, 1920.

Specific quotes from:

(1) Paragraph 1

Cannot locate

(2) Paragraph 3

(a) "wrote Miss Mitford"

       To Sir William Elford, Feb. 19, 1825;
repr. in L'Estrange (see below), Vol.
II.

(b) M. Mitford to Rev. William Harness, May
2, 1834; repr. in *ibid.*, Vol. III.

(c) M. Mitford, *Recollections of a Literary
Life.*

(See "The Wrong Way of Reading.")

"[H]ave" should read "had."

(3) Paragraph 4

(a) "[Miss Mitford] exclaimed"

To Emily Jephson, May 31, 1837; repr.
in *The Life of Mary Russell Mitford ...
from Her Letters*, ed. by A.G. L'Estrange.
3 vol. Richard Bentley, 1870. Vol. III.

(b) "she said"

Paraphrase of M. Mitford to Dr. George
Mitford, July 5, 1811

(See "The Wrong Way of Reading.")

(c) "she observed"

Paraphrase of M. Mitford to "a friend,"
Jan. 7, 1855; repr. in L'Estrange (see
above), Vol. III.

Important Allusions (mentioned by Hill):

Works by M. Mitford:

(1) *Rienzi.*   (Orig. 1828)

(2) *Our Village.* (Orig. 1824)

Passing Allusion (mentioned by M. Mitford):

Jane Austen

GORKY ON TOLSTOI (1920)   C204

    Obvious Source:

        Maxim Gorky, *Reminiscences of Leo Nicolayevitch Tolstoi*, [trans. by S.S. Koteliansky and Leonard Woolf]. Hogarth Pr., 1920.

    Passing Allusions (mentioned by Gorky):

        (1) Works by Tolstoi:

            (a) *The Kreutzer Sonata*. (Orig. 1889-90)

            (b) *War and Peace*. (Orig. 1868)

        (2) Sviatogor (described in footnote as "A hero in Russian legend, brave and wild and self-willed, like a child")

- -

GREAT MEN'S HOUSES (1932)   C333.1

    Important Allusions:

        Miscellaneous British writers: Jane Welsh Carlyle, Thomas Carlyle, John Keats

    Passing Allusions:

        Miscellaneous English writers: Samuel Taylor Coleridge, Charles Dickens, Samuel Johnson, William Shakespeare

- -

GREAT NAMES: GEORGE ELIOT (1819-1880) (1921) C216.1

    Important Allusions:

        Works by Eliot:

        (1) *Scenes of Clerical Life* (1858)

        (2) *Adam Bede* (1859)

        (3) *The Mill on the Floss* (1860)

(4) *Silas Marner* (1861)

(5) *Middlemarch* (1871-72)

(6) *Romola* (1863)

(7) *Daniel Deronda* (1876)

Passing Allusions:

(1) George Henry Lewes

(2) Mrs. Poyser (character in *Adam Bede*)

- -

GUESTS AND MEMORIES (1925)   C260.2

Obvious Source:

Una Taylor, *Guests and Memories: Annals of a Seaside Villa*. Oxford U. Pr., 1925.

Important Allusion (mentioned by U. Taylor):

Henry Taylor

Passing Allusions (mentioned by U. Taylor):

Miscellaneous British writers: Thomas Carlyle, Benjamin Jowett, Robert Louis Stevenson, Alfred Lord Tennyson

- -

HEARTS OF CONTROVERSY (1917)   C90

Obvious Source:

Alice Meynell, *Hearts of Controversy*. Burns and Oates, 1917.

(1) Specific essays quoted from:

(a) *Re* Charlotte Brontë:

"Charlotte and Emily Brontë." (Orig. 1911)

(b) *Re* Charles Dickens:

"Dickens as a Man of Letters." (Orig. 1912, as "Notes of a Reader of Dickens")

(c) *Re* Alfred Lord Tennyson:

"Some Thoughts of a Reader of Tennyson." (Orig. 1910, as "Tennyson")

(2) Essay mentioned but not quoted from:

Re Algernon Charles Swinburne:

"Swinburne's Lyrical Poetry." (Orig. 1909)

Passing Allusions (mentioned by Meynell):

Miscellaneous English writers: Lascelles Abercrombie, Matthew Arnold, Charles Lamb, William Makepeace Thackeray

- -

HENLEY'S CRITICISM (1921)   C215

Obvious Source:

William Ernest Henley, *Essays*. Macmillan, 1920.

(1) Specific essays quoted from:

(a) "Henry Fielding." (Orig. 1903)

Both quotes, paragraph 1, are from here.

(b) "Robert Burns." (Orig. 1896)

Quotes, paragraphs 3 and 4, are from here.

(2) Essays mentioned but not quoted from:

(a) *Re* Tobias Smollett:

"Smollett." (Orig. 1899)

(b) "William Hazlitt." (Orig. 1902-04)

(c) "Lord Byron's World." (Orig. 1897)

Important Allusions:

(1) Mentioned by Henley: Robert Louis Stevenson

(2) "Carlyle's Boswell"

Thomas Carlyle, "Boswell's Life of Johnson,"
Fraser's Magazine, 5 (May 1832), 379-413;
repr. in e.g., Carlyle, *The Collected Works
of* ... Poss. ed.: 16 vol. Chapman and Hall,
1857-58. Vol. IV.

This is listed in Holleyman; it belonged to
Leslie Stephen.

(3) "Macaulay's Warren Hastings"

Thomas Babington Macaulay, "Warren Hastings,"
Edinburgh Review, 74 (Oct. 1841), 160ff.;
repr. in, e.g., Macaulay, *Critical and
Historical Essays* ...(Orig. 1843) Poss. ed.:
Ed. by A.J. Grieve. Everyman's Ed. 2 vol.
J.M. Dent, 1907. Vol. I.

This is listed in Holleyman, along with two
earlier editions (1852, 1864).

Passing Allusions (mentioned by Henley):

(1) Fielding, *The History of Tom Jones*. (Orig.
1749)

(2) Miscellaneous British writers: Robert Browning, Samuel Taylor Coleridge, Austin Dobson,
George Eliot [pseud. of Mary Ann Evans], Edward Gibbon, Thomas Gray, Sir Walter Scott,
Leslie Stephen, William Makepeace Thackeray

- -

THE HIGHER COURT (1920)   C191

Supportive Source:

Margaret E.M. Young, *The Higher Court*. (Publ.
later by Burns, Oates, 1931)

THE HOUSE OF LYME (1917)   C70

    Obvious Source:

        Lady Newton [Evelyn Legh], *The House of Lyme*
        from Its Foundation to the End of the Eighteenth
        Century. Heinemann, 1917.

- -

THE HOUSE OF MIRTH (1905)   C2.7

    Obvious Source: Reading notes
                                               B1a
        Edith Wharton, *The House of Mirth.* Macmillan,
        1905.

- -

THE HOUSE OF SHADOWS (1906)   C3.6

    Obvious Source: Reading notes
                                             B1a
        R[eginald] J. Farrer, *The House of Shadows.* Ed-
        ward Arnold, 1906.

- -

HOW SHOULD ONE READ A BOOK? (1926)   C277

    Supportive Sources:

        (1) Daniel Defoe, *Robinson Crusoe.* (Orig. 1719)

        (2) Jane Austen, *Emma.* (Orig. 1816)

            Characters, p. 35, are from here.

    Important Allusions:

        (1) Miscellaneous English poets: John Keats,
            William Shakespeare

        (2) Various novels:

            (a) William Makepeace Thackeray, *Vanity Fair.*
                (Orig. 1848)

      (b) Samuel Richardson, *Clarissa Harlowe.*
          (Orig. 1747-48)

      (c) Leo Tolstoi, *Anna Karenina.* (Orig.
          1873-77)

Passing Allusions:

      (1) John Milton, *Paradise Lost.* (Orig. 1667)

      (2) Thomas Hardy, *Tess of the D'Urbervilles.*
          (Orig. 1891)

      (3) Miscellaneous writers: Joseph Conrad, John
          Dryden, Gustave Flaubert, Samuel Johnson,
          Rudyard Kipling, George Meredith, Thomas
          Love Peacock, Sir Walter Scott, Anthony
          Trollope

- -

IMITATIVE ESSAYS (1918)   C108

Obvious Source:

    J[ohn] C[ollings] Squire, *The Gold Tree.* Martin
    Secker, 1917.

    Specific stories quoted from:

    (1) "The Gold Tree"

       First quote is from here.

    (2) "we hastily turn the page"

       "The Walled Garden"

    (3) "A quotation ... will show"

       Ibid.

THE IMMORTAL ISLES (1927)   C280.1

    Obvious Source:

        Seton Gordon, *The Immortal Isles*. Williams and
        Norgate, 1926.

- -

AN IMPERFECT LADY (1920)*   C192

    Obvious Source:

        Constance Hill, *Mary Russell Mitford and Her
        Surroundings*. John Lane, 1920.

    Passing Allusions:

        (1) Miscellaneous women writers:

            (a) Mentioned by Hill: Jane Austen, Mary
                Martha Sherwood

            (b) the Brontës, Elizabeth Barrett Browning,
                Fanny Burney, Maria Edgeworth, George
                Eliot [pseud. of Mary Ann Evans], Har-
                riet Martineau, George Sand [pseud. of
                Amadine Aurora Lucie Dupin, Baroness Du-
                devant], Sappho

        (2) Mentioned by Hill:

            (a) "Mr. Crissy"

                J. Crissy published Mitford's first "col-
                lected works," *The Works of M.R.* [*sic*]
                Mitford, Prose and Verse. Philadelphia:
                N.p., 1840.

            (b) "*Adam's Geography*"

                Alexander Adam, *A Summary of Geography
                and History Both Ancient and Modern*.
                (Orig. 1794)

*   This essay contributed to "Miss Mitford" in *Common Read-
    er I*.

AN IMPRESSION OF GISSING(1923)   C236

Obvious Sources:

> (1) May Yates, *George Gissing: An Appreciation*.
> Manchester: Manchester U. Pr., 1923.

> (2) [Morley Roberts], *The Private Life of Henry
> Maitland*. Nash and Grayson, 1923. (Orig.
> 1912)

Important Allusions:

Works by Gissing:

> (1) *New Grub Street*. (Orig. 1891)

> (2) *Born in Exile*. (Orig. 1892)

> (3) *The Private Papers of Henry Ryecroft*. (Orig.
> 1903)

> > Woolf reviewed this for *Guardian*, Feb. 13,
> > 1907, pp. 282-83.

Passing Allusions:

Miscellaneous English writers:

> (1) Mentioned by Yates: Samuel Butler, Charles
> Dickens, Dr. Samuel Johnson, William Shake-
> speare

> (2) Jane Austen

- -

IN GOOD COMPANY (1917)   C73

Obvious Source:

> Coulson Kernahan, *In Good Company*. John Lane,
> 1917.

Important Allusions (mentioned by Kernahan):

> (1) Algernon Charles Swinburne

> (2) "[Theodore] Watts-Dunton ... left only two
> published volumes behind him"

   (a) *The Coming of Love and Other Poems.*
       (Orig. 1898)

   (b) *Aylwin. A Novel.* (Orig. 1899)

Passing Allusions:

   Miscellaneous English writers: George Borrow,
   Alfred Lord Tennyson (mentioned by Kernahan)

- -

IN MEMORIAM: CAROLINE EMELIA STEPHEN (1909) C32.1

   Supportive Source:

       Caroline Emelia Stephen, *Quaker Strongholds.*
       (Orig. 1890)

   Important Allusions:

       Other works by C. Stephen

       (1) *The Service of the Poor.* (Orig. 1871)

       (2) *The First Sir James Stephen.* (Orig. 1906)

       (3) *Light Arising.* (Orig. 1908)

- -

IN MY ANECDOTAGE (1925)   C265.3

   Obvious Source:

       W.G. Elliot, *In My Anecdotage.* Philip Allan,
       1925.

- -

IS THIS POETRY? (1919)*   C155.1

   Obvious Sources:

       (1) J[ohn] M[iddleton] Murry, *The Critic in
           Judgment.* Hogarth Pr., 1919.

Specific quote from:

"The Critic in Judgment or Belshazzar of⁻
Baronscourt." (Orig. 1913) Ll. 110-16.

(2) T[homas] S[tearns] Eliot, *Poems*. Hogarth
Pr., 1919.

  (a) Specific poems quoted from (paragraph
  4):

  (i) "Mr. Eliot's Sunday Morning Service." (Orig. 1918)

  (ii) "Sweeney Among the Nightingales."
  (Orig. 1918)

  (b) Specific poem mentioned but not quoted
  from:

  "The Hippopotamus." (Orig. 1917)

Supportive Source:

  Re P[ublius] Papinius Statius

  Cannot locate

  [The "Silver Age" of Roman literature covered
  roughly 1-150 A.D.]

Important Allusion:

  Eliot, "The Love Song of J. Alfred Prufrock."
  (Orig. 1915)

Passing Allusions:

  Miscellaneous writers: Sir Thomas Browne, Plato

* B.J. Kirkpatrick identifies this (p. 150) as a joint
review by Virginia and Leonard Woolf, with the latter
"handling" the part on Eliot.
- -

JANE AUSTEN (1913)*   C49.2

Obvious Sources:

  (1) William and Richard A. Austen-Leigh, *Life
  and Letters of Jane Austen*. Smith, Elder,
  1913.

Specific quotes from:

(a) "little Philadelphia Austen [*sic*] ...
     describes Jane"

     Philadelphia Walter to her brother
     James, July 23, 1788

(b) "Mrs. Mitford ... and ... Miss Mitford's
     ... anonymous friend"

     Mary Russell Mitford to Sir William El-
     ford, Apr. 3, 1815; repr. in, e.g., *The
     Life of Mary Russell Mitford, Told* ...
     in Letters to Her Friends.

     (See "The Wrong Way of Reading.")

(c) "Marianne Knight ... recalled not very
     many years ago"

     Apparently oral report

(d) "the words addressed to the nephew"

     Jane Austen to J. E[dward] Austen-Leigh,
     [Dec. 16, 1816]

(2) Sybil G. Brinton, *Old Friends and New Faces.*
    Holden and Hardingham, 1913.

Supportive Sources:

(1) Works by Austen:

(a) *Mansfield Park.* (Orig. 1814)

     Paragraph 3, quote 2, is from here.

(b) *Emma.* (Orig. 1816)

     Third paragraph from end, first quote,
     is from here.

(c) *Pride and Prejudice.* (Orig. 1813)

     Third paragraph from end, quotes 2-3,
     are from here.

(2) "Professor Bradley in his lecture to the
    English Association"

    Andrew Cecil Bradley, "Jane Austen: A Lec-
    ture," in *Essays and Studies by Members of
    the English Association*, 2 (1911), 7-36.

Important Allusions:

(1) "In 1870 the memoir by her nephew"

James Austen-Leigh, *A Memoir of Jane Austen*. Richard Bentley, 1870.

(2) "the letters which appeared in Lord Brabourne's two volumes"

Letters of Jane Austen, ed. by Edward, Lord Brabourne. 2 vol. Richard Bentley, 1884.

(3) "So lately as 1870 there was only one complete edition of the novels."

(a) Standard Novels ser., Nos. XXIII, XXV, XXVII, XXVIII, XXX. 5 vol. Richard Bentley, 1833. (Frequent reprints)

(b) In 1870: *Jane Austen's Works*. 5 vol. Chapman and Hall.

(4) "[Austen's] six neat volumes"

See three titles listed above; also:

(a) *Persuasion*. (Orig. 1818)

(b) *Sense and Sensibility*. (Orig. 1811)

(c) *Northanger Abbey*. (Orig. 1818, printed with *Persuasion*)

(d) Plus: *The Watsons*. (Orig. publ. 1871)

Passing Allusions:

Various Austen characters not specifically at-
tributed by Woolf: *Emma*--Mrs. Norris, William, Emma Woodhouse, Mr. Woodhouse; *Pride and Preju-
dice*--Mr. Collins, Sir William Lucas; *Mansfield Park*--Lady Bertram, Mrs. Chapman; *The Watsons*--Miss Fanny Carr; *Sense and Sensibility*--Elinor Dashwood; *Northanger Abbey*--Mrs. Allen

* This essay contributed to "Jane Austen" in *Common Reader I*.

JANE AUSTEN AT SIXTY (1923)*   C241

Obvious Sources:

> *"The Works of Jane Austen"*
>
> I.e., *The Novels of Jane Austen*, edited by R.W. Chapman. 5 vol. Oxford: Clarendon, 1923. (Orig. in this ed. 1870)
>
> Specifically mentioned:
>
> *Persuasion*. (Orig. 1818)

Supportive Source:

> "wrote Mr. Austen Leigh"
>
> James Austen-Leigh, *A Memoir of Jane Austen*. Richard Bentley, 1870.
>
> Quote *re* Dr. [William] Whewell and final quote are also from here.

Passing Allusions:

> (1) George Eliot [pseud. of Mary Ann Evans], *Middlemarch*. (Orig. 1872-73)
>
> (2) Austen's "six famous novels":
>
>> (a) *Pride and Prejudice*. (Orig. 1813)
>>
>> (b) *Mansfield Park*. (Orig. 1814)
>>
>> (c) *Persuasion*.
>>
>> (d) *Sense and Sensibility*. (Orig. 1811)
>>
>> (e) *Emma*. (Orig. 1816)
>>
>> (f) *Northanger Abbey*. (Orig. 1818)
>
> (3) Various characters in *Persuasion*: Sir Walter and Miss Anne Elliott [*sic*; i.e., Elliot] Admiral Croft; Mrs. Musgrove
>
> (4) Miscellaneous novelists: Henry James, Marcel Proust

---

*   This essay contributed to "Jane Austen" in *Common Reader I*.

JOHN ADDINGTON SYMONDS (1925)   C261

    Obvious Source:

        Margaret Symonds, *Out of the Past.* New York:
        Charles Scribner's; London: Murray, 1925.

        Specific letters quoted from:

        (1) First quote

            Cannot locate

        (2) Second quote

            J.A. Symonds to Margaret Symonds, [Aug. 10,
            1891]

        (3) "he wrote"; "he held"

            Same to same, [Oct. 19, 1892]

    Important Allusion (mentioned by M. Symonds):

        John Addington Symonds, *History of the Renais-
        sance in Italy.* (Orig. 1875-86)

    Passing Allusions (mentioned by M. Symonds):

        Miscellaneous English writers: Matthew Arnold,
        Arthur Hugh Clough, Benjamin Jowett

- -

JOHN DAVIDSON (1917)   C82

    Stated Impulse:

        Hayim Fineman, *John Davidson. A Study of the Re-
        lation of His Ideas to His Poetry.* Philadelphia:
        N.p., 1917.

    Inferred Sources:

        "Mr. Fineman sends us back to Davidson's books"

        (1) *The Testament of John Davidson.* Grant
            Richards, 1898.

            Quotes 2-4, paragraph 2, are from here; also
            first quote, paragraph 3.

(2) "the tragic preface in which [Davidson] stated"

Preface to *Fleet Street and Other Poems*. Grant Richards, 1909.

(3) In paragraph 3:

(a) "[Davidson] said"

The Testament of a Man Forbid. Grant Richards, 1901.

(b) "a first-rate piece of description"

"The Crystal Palace." In *Fleet Street and Other Poems* (see above).

(4) In paragraph 4:

(a) "On the one hand we have"

"St. George's Day." In *Fleet Street Eclogues*. John Lane, 1893.

(b) "on the other [hand]"

"The Outcast." In *The Last Ballad and Other Poems*. John Lane, 1899.

(c) "Davidson ... sings"

The Testament of a Man Forbid (see above).

Important Allusion (mentioned by Fineman):

Davidson, *Ballads and Songs*. John Lane, 1894.

Passing Allusions:

Miscellaneous writers:

(1) Dante Alighieri, George Gissing, John Milton

(2) Mentioned by Davidson: William Shakespeare

JULIA MARGARET CAMERON (1926)   B5

    Important Allusions:

        (1) William Makepeace Thackeray, "On a Good-
            looking Young Lady," *Punch*, 18 (June 8,
            1850), 223.

        (2) Sir Henry Taylor

    Passing Allusions:

        (1) Miscellaneous British writers: Thomas Car-
            lyle, Aubrey de Vere, Benjamin Jowett, John
            Ruskin

        (2) Alfred Lord Tennyson, *Maud*. (Orig. 1855)

- -

LADY FANSHAWE'S MEMOIRS (1907)   C6

    Obvious Source:

        The Memoirs of Anne Lady Fanshawe, ... *1600-72*,
        [ed. by Herbert C. Fanshawe]. John Lane, 1907.
        (Orig. 1829)

    Passing Allusions:

        (1) Mentioned by Lady Anne:

            Edmund Spenser, *The Faery Queene*. (Orig.
            1590, 1596)

        (2) Miscellaneous English diarists (mentioned
            by H. Fanshawe): John Evelyn, Samuel Pepys

- -

LADY OTTOLINE MORRELL (1938)   C354

    Passing Allusions:

        Miscellaneous English poets: John Keats, Percy
        Bysshe Shelley

LADY RITCHIE (1919)   C142

Supportive Sources:

> (1) Works by Lady Anne Ritchie [b. Thackeray]:
>
>> (a) *The Story of Elizabeth.* (Orig. 1863)
>>
>> (b) *Old Kensington.* (Orig. 1873)
>>
>> Poss. ed.: In *The Works of Anne Isabella Thackeray.* 8 vol. Smith, Elder, 1875-76.
>>
>> This is listed in Holleyman Addendum.
>>
>> (c) "Here is Charlotte Brontë"; "[here is] George Sand"
>>
>> Ritchie, *Chapters from Some Memoirs.* Macmillan, 1894.
>
> (2) "As Leslie Stephen ... wrote of her"
>
>> Stephen, *The Mausoleum Book, 1895.* In MS. (Later published as *Sir Leslie Stephen's Mausoleum Book*, ed. by Alan Bell. Oxford: Clarendon, 1977.)

Important Allusion:

> Anne Isabella Thackeray [Lady Ritchie], *The Village on the Cliff.* (Orig. 1867)

Passing Allusions:

> Miscellaneous English novelists: Jane Austen (mentioned by L. Stephen), George Borrow, George Eliot [pseud. of Mary Ann Evans], Elizabeth Gaskell, Anthony Trollope

- -

LANDOR IN LITTLE (1919)   C170

Obvious Source:

> Walter Savage Landor, *A Day-Book of ...* , chosen by John Bailey. Oxford: Clarendon; London: Milford, 1919.

Specific quotes from:

(1) "Mr. Bailey['s] ... discriminating introduction"

First 4 quotes are from here.

(2) From various works by Landor:

(a) "Aesop and Rhodope." First publ. in Landor, *Works*. 2 vol. Moxon, 1846. Vol. II.

(b) "Leofric and Godiva." In Landor, *Imaginary Conversations*. Vol. IV. (Orig. 1829)

There should be ellipses between "beloved" and "Sad."

(c) "Lord Brooke and Sir Philip Sidney." In *ibid.*, Vol. I. (Orig. 1824)

(d) "Epicurus, Leontion, and Ternissa." In *ibid.*, Vol. V. (Orig. 1829)

(e) "William Penn and Lord Peterborough." In *ibid.*

(f) *Pericles and Aspasia*. 2 vol. Saunders and Otley, 1836.

(g) Landor to Constantine Henry Phipps, Marquis of Normanby, Dec. 30, 1858; repr. in Landor, *Letters of* ... , ed. by Stephen Wheeler. Duckworth, 1899.

Passing Allusions:

Miscellaneous writers:

(1) Mentioned by Landor: Andrew Marvell, Philip Melancthon, Torquato Tasso

(2) Mentioned by Bailey: Aesop, Richard Porson, Robert Southey

THE LAST DAYS OF MARIE ANTOINETTE (1907)   See p. 179, KP

Obvious Source:

Lenôtre [pseud. of Louis Léon Théodore Gosselin], ed., *The Last Days of Marie Antoinette*, trans. by Mrs. Rodolph Stawell. Heinemann, 1907.

Passing Allusion (mentioned by Claud Moëlle):

Gaius Cornelius Tacitus

[Moëlle's "Narrative" is one of twenty comprising Lenôtre's collection.]

- -

LAUGHTER AND TEARS (1926)   C276.1

Obvious Source:

Jerome K. Jerome, *My Life and Times*. Hodder and Stoughton, 1926.

Specific quote from:

"The *Morning Post* said" (London newspaper, 1772-1936)

N.d. given; quote should begin with "an"

Important Allusions (mentioned by Jerome):

(1) Jerome, *Three Men in a Boat*. (Orig. 1889)

(2) *Punch* (periodical, 1841-present)

Passing Allusions (mentioned by Jerome):

Miscellaneous English writers: Max Beerbohm, W[illiam] W[ymark] Jacobs, H[erbert] G[eorge] Wells

THE LETTER KILLETH (1905)   C2.4

Obvious Source: Reading notes
                                       B1a
        A. C[unnick] Inchbold, *The Letter Killeth.*
        Partridge, 1905.

- -

LETTERS AND JOURNALS OF ANNE CHALMERS (1924) C244.4

Obvious Source:

        Letters and Journals of Anne Chalmers, ed. by
        Her Daughter [Matilda Grace Blackie]. Chelsea
        Publ. Co., 1923. (Orig. 1922)

Passing Allusions (mentioned by Chalmers):

        Miscellaneous English poets: Lord Byron, Samuel
        Taylor Coleridge

- -

LETTERS OF CHRISTINA ROSSETTI (1908)   C19

Obvious Source:

        Christina Rossetti, *The Family Letters of ...* ,
        ed. by William Michael Rossetti. Brown, Lang-
        ham, 1908.

        Specific letters quoted from:

        (1) Paragraph 2

            (a) First quote

                C. Rossetti to W.M. Rossetti, [Aug. 25,
                1849] and Aug. 18, 1858. ("Letter" thus
                an amalgam of two; there should be ellip-
                ses after "failure.")

            (b) "she wrote when young"

                Same to same, [Nov. 13, 1855]

        (2) Paragraph 3

(a) "on the death of her grandmother"

C. Rossetti to Frances Rossetti, Apr. 18, 1853

(b) "in D.G. Rossetti's [*sic*] phrase"

I.e., C. Rossetti *to* D[ante] G[abriel] Rossetti, Aug. 4, 1881

(c) "did she not answer"

Same to same, [Apr. (?), 1870]

(d) "she was bold to claim"

Same to same, Jan. 1, [1877]

Important Allusion:

C. Rossetti, *Goblin Market*. (Orig. 1862)

- -

THE LETTERS OF JANE WELSH CARLYLE (1905)   C2.1

Inferred Sources:

(1) Jane Welsh Carlyle, *New Letters and Memorials of*, ed. by Alexander Carlyle, w/intro. by James Crichton-Browne. 2 vol. John Lane, 1903.

This is listed in Holleyman.

Specific quote from:

"wrote Carlyle" (quoted by Crichton-Browne)

Thomas Carlyle, Journal, Dec. (?), 1868

Paragraph 2, quote 3, is also from here.

(2) "the first [*sic*] volume of the 'Letters and Memorials'"

I.e., *Letters and Memorials of Jane Welsh Carlyle*, ed. by Thomas Carlyle and J.A. Froude. 3 vol. Longmans, 1883.

This is listed in Holleyman Addendum II; it belonged to Leslie Stephen.

Specific quotes from:

(a) Paragraph 2:

   (i) Quote 1

      J. Carlyle to Thomas Carlyle,
      Sept. 12(?), 1843. Vol. I.

   (ii) Quote 2

      Same to same, July 26, 1849. Vol.
      II.

(b) Paragraph 3:

   (i) Quote 1

      J. Carlyle to Susan Stirling, Jan.
      8, 1841. Vol. I.

   (ii) Quote 2

      J. Carlyle to Mary Russell, Dec.
      30, 1858. Vol. II.

      First quote, paragraph 5, is also
      from here.

(c) Paragraph 4:

   (i) "Take, for instance, a scene from
      her notebook"

      J. Carlyle, notebook, Apr. 13,
      1845; should read "the prince of
      critics and the prince of dandies."
      Vol. I.

   (ii) "Then she goes on" (quotes 2-9)

      Ibid., Apr. (?) [between Apr. 13
      and 27], 1845. Vol. I.

(d) Paragraph 5:

   (i) Quote 2

      J. Carlyle, Narrative in MS, Aug.
      2, 1849. Vol. II.

   (ii) Quotes 3-4

      J. Carlyle to Mary Russell, Dec.
      30, 1845. Vol. I.

(iii) Quote 5

J. Carlyle to Jane Aitken, Apr. (?), 1846. Vol. I.

(iv) Quote 6

Same to same, May (?), 1849. Vol. II; "the" should not be in quotes

Supportive Source:

"as Mr. Froude says" (paragraph 3)

J[ames] A[nthony] Froude, *Thomas Carlyle: A History of His Life in London, 1834-1881.* 2 vol. Longmans, 1884. Vol. I.

This is listed in Holleyman.

Passing Allusion:

Charles Lamb

- -

THE LETTERS OF MARY RUSSELL MITFORD (1925)   C261.2

Obvious Source:

Mary Russell Mitford, *The Letters of ...* , sel. by R. Brimley Johnson. Bodley Head, 1925.

Passing Allusions:

Miscellaneous writers: William Cowper, Sir Walter Scott (mentioned by Mitford), Marie de Sévigné

- -

THE LIFE AND LAST WORDS OF WILFRID EWART (1924)   C246.5

Obvious Source:

Stephen Graham, *The Life and Last Words of Wilfrid Ewart.* Putnam, 1924.

Passing Allusion (mentioned by Graham):

"one novel of great promise"

Ewart, *Love and Strife*. In MS. [Later published
by Richards, 1936.]

- -

THE LIMITS OF PERFECTION (1919)   C174

Obvious Source:

Max Beerbohm, *Seven Men*. Heinemann, 1919.

Specific stories mentioned:

(1) "James Pethel." (Orig. 1912)

(2) "the story of ... the week-end party at Keeb"

"Hilary Maltby and Stephen Braxton." (Orig.
1917)

(3) "Enoch Soames." (Orig. 1912)

(4) "'Savonarola' Brown." (Orig. 1917)

Passing Allusions:

(1) Mentioned by Beerbohm:

The Yellow Book. (Periodical, 1894-97)

(2) Miscellaneous English writers: Charles Dickens (mentioned by Beerbohm), Charles Lamb

- -

LONDON REVISITED (1916)   C57

Obvious Source:

E[dward] V[errall] Lucas, *London Revisited*. Methuen, 1916.

Passing Allusion (mentioned by Lucas):

Charles Lamb

LONE MARIE (1905)   C2.5

    Obvious Source: Reading notes
                                                B1a
        W[illiam] E[dward] Norris, *Lone Marie*. Macmil-
        lan, 1905.

    Important Allusion:

        Henry James

- -

LORD JIM (1917)   C81

    Obvious Source:

        Joseph Conrad, *Lord Jim*. New ed. Dent, 1917.
        (Orig. 1900)

    Important Allusions:

        Works by Conrad:

        (1) *The Shadow Line*. Dent, 1917.

        (2) *The Heart of Darkness*. (Orig. 1902)

        (3) *Youth*. (Orig. 1902)

        (4) *Typhoon*. (Orig. 1902)

        (5) "fragment of Reminiscences"

            Some Reminiscences. Eveleigh Nash, 1912.

    Passing Allusion:

        Fyodor Dostoevsky

- -

LOUD LAUGHTER (1918)   C112

    Obvious Source:

        Stephen Leacock, *Frenzied Fiction*. John Lane,
        1918.

(1) Specific essay quoted from:

"Back from the Land"

(2) Essays mentioned but not quoted from:

(a) "The Prophet in Our Midst"

(b) "To Nature and Back Again"

Passing Allusions:

Various characters: Falstaff; Mrs. [Sarah] Gamp (in Charles Dickens, *Martin Chuzzlewit* [1844])

- -

LOUISE DE LA VALLIERE (1908)   C26

Obvious Source:

J[ules] Lair, *Louise de la Vallière*.... [4th ed.] Paris: N.p., 1908.

[Although an English ed., trans. by Ethel C. Mayne, was also published in 1908, by Hutchinson, Woolf used the French ed., as her quotes in that language show.]

- -

MADELEINE (1919)   C169

Obvious Source: Reading notes
                                       B2i
Hope Mirrlees, *Madeleine, One of Love's Jansen-ists*. Collins, 1919.

- -

MAINLY VICTORIAN (1925)   C260.3

Obvious Source:

Stewart M. Ellis, *Mainly Victorian*. Hutchinson, 1925.

Passing Allusion (mentioned by Ellis):

The London Mercury (periodical, 1919-39)

- -

THE MAKING OF MICHAEL (1905)   C2.10

Obvious Source: Reading notes
                                        B1a
        Mrs. [Amy D.] Fred Reynolds, *The Making of Mi-
        chael*. George Allen, 1905.

- -

MARIE ELIZABETH TOWNELEY (1924)   C246.31

Obvious Source:

        [Marie, des Saints Anges], *Mary Elizabeth Towne-
        ley ... A Memoir*, w/preface by the Bishop of
        Southwark. Burns, Oates, 1924.

- -

MARY ELIZABETH HALDANE (1926)   C270.1

Obvious Source:

        *Mary Elizabeth Haldane, A Record of a Hundred
        Years*, ed. by Her Daughter [Elizabeth Sanderson
        Haldane]. Hodder and Stoughton, 1924(?).

- -

MATURITY AND IMMATURITY (1919)   C176

Obvious Sources:

        (1) Pamela Glenconner, *Edward Wyndham Tennant: A
            Memoir*. Lane, 1919.

        (2) *Joyce Kilmer*, ed. with a memoir by Robert
            Cortes Holliday. Hodder and Stoughton, 1919.

Important Allusion (mentioned by Glenconner):

Edward Wyndham Tennant, "The Mad Soldier."

Passing Allusions:

(1) Miscellaneous British writers:

(a) Mentioned by Glenconner: Siegfried Sassoon, Alfred Lord Tennyson

(b) Mentioned by Holliday: Hilaire Belloc, G[ilbert] K[eith] Chesterton, Gerard Manley Hopkins, Charles Lamb, Walter Pater, Sir Walter Scott

(2) Mentioned by Holliday:

Thomas Gray, "Elegy Written in a Country Churchyard." (Orig. 1750)

(3) Kilmer, *Carnival* [*sic*]

Cannot locate; Woolf may mean Kilmer, *The Circus*. New York: L.J. Gomme, 1916.

- -

MELBA (1925)   C269.2

Obvious Source:

Nellie Melba, *Memories and Melodies*. Thornton Butterworth, 1925.

Passing Allusion:

"Home, Sweet Home"

Popular song from *Clari* (1823); music by Sir Henry Rowley Bishop, words by John Howard Payne

- -

MELODIOUS MEDITATIONS (1917)   C65

Obvious Source:

Henry Dwight Sedgwick, *An Apology for Old Maids,* w/preface by Owen Wister. Macmillan, 1916.

Specific essays quoted from:

(1) "On Being Ill." (Orig. 1916)

(2) First paragraph, last quote

"A Forsaken God." (Orig. 1916)

Supportive Source:

Walt Whitman, *Leaves of Grass*. "Preface to first edition" (1855).

Poss. ed.: Philadelphia: D. McKay, 1884.

This is listed in Holleyman Addendum.

Final quote is from here.

Passing Allusions:

(1) *The Gentleman's Magazine* (periodical, 1731-1907)

(2) Mentioned by Sedgwick: Johann Wolfgang von Goethe

- -

THE MEMOIRS OF LADY DOROTHY NEVILL (1908)   C23

Obvious Source:

Lady Dorothy Nevill, *The Memoirs* [*sic*; i.e., *Reminiscences*] *of* ... , ed. by Ralph Nevill. E. Arnold, 1907. (Orig. 1906)

Passing Allusions:

Miscellaneous writers: John Keats, Sappho, Mrs. [Mary Augusta] Humphry Ward

- -

MEMORIES (1928)   C305.2

Obvious Source:

Julian Hawthorne, *Shapes That Pass*. Murray, 1928.

Important Allusions (mentioned by J. Hawthorne):

Miscellaneous writers: Robert Browning, Elizabeth Barrett Browning, Henry James

Passing Allusions (mentioned by J. Hawthorne):

Miscellaneous writers: Lord Byron, Nathaniel
Hawthorne

- -

MEMORIES AND NOTES (1928)   C297.1

Obvious Source:

Anthony Hope, *Memories and Notes*.   Hutchinson,
1927.

Passing Allusion (mentioned by Hope):

Benjamin Jowett

- -

MEMORIES OF A MILITANT (1924)   C256.1

Obvious Source:

Annie Kenney, *Memories of a Militant*.   Arnold,
1924.

Passing Allusion (mentioned by Kenney):

François Marie Arouet de Voltaire

- -

MEMORIES OF MEREDITH (1919)   C180

Obvious Source:

Lady [Alice Mary] Butcher, *Memories of George
Meredith, O.M.* Constable, 1919.

Specific quote from:

Meredith, *Vittoria*.   (Orig. 1867)

Important Allusions:

(1) Meredith, "The Woods of Westermain."   (Orig.
1883)

    (2) Miscellaneous women writers (mentioned by
        Lady Butcher): Jane Austen, Charlotte Yonge

Passing Allusions (mentioned by Lady Butcher):

    (1) John Keble, *The Christian Year*. (Orig. 1827)

    (2) Guy de Maupassant

- -

THE METHOD OF HENRY JAMES (1918)   C138

Obvious Source:

    Joseph Warren Beach, *The Method of Henry James*.
    New Haven, Conn.: Yale U. Pr.; London: Milford,
    1918.

    Specific quote from:

    James, Preface to *The Awkward Age*. (Orig. 1899)
    Vol. 9 of "New York Edition." 24 vol. Macmil-
    lan, 1908-09.

Important Allusions (mentioned by Beach):

    Works by James:

    (1) *The Wings of the Dove*. (Orig. 1902)

    (2) *The Ambassadors*. (Orig. 1903)

    (3) *The Golden Bowl*.   (Orig. 1904)

    (4) *The Tragic Muse*. (Orig. 1889)

- -

THE MILLS OF THE GODS (1920)   C196

Obvious Source:

    Elizabeth Robins, *The Mills of the Gods*. Thorn-
    ton Butterworth, 1920.

A MINOR DOSTOEVSKY (1917)   C88

Obvious Source:

Fyodor Dostoevsky, *The Gambler and Other Stories*,
trans. by Constance Garnett. Heinemann, 1917.

Specific stories mentioned:

(1) "Poor People." (Orig. 1845)

(2) "The Landlady." (Orig. 1847)

Important Allusions:

Novels by Dostoevsky:

(1) *The Idiot*. (Orig. 1882)

(2) *The Brothers Karamazov*. (Orig. 1880)

Passing Allusion:

Leo Tolstoy

- -

MORE CARLYLE LETTERS (1909)   C31

Obvious Source:

*The Love Letters of Thomas Carlyle and Jane
Welsh*, ed. by Alexander Carlyle. 2 vol. Lane,
1909.

Important Allusions:

(1) James Anthony Froude, *My Relations with Carlyle*. (Orig. 1886)

(2) Jane Welsh Carlyle, *New Letters and Memorials
of* ... , ed. by Alexander Carlyle. 2 vol.
John Lane, 1903.

This is listed in Holleyman. Woolf reviewed
it for *Guardian*, Aug. 2, 1905, p. 1295.
(See "The Letters of Jane Welsh Carlyle.")

Passing Allusions (mentioned by Jane and Thomas):

Miscellaneous writers: Lord Byron, Anne Louise
de Staël

MR. BENNETT AND MRS. BROWN (1924)   C240

Inferred Impulse:

"The other day Mr. Arnold Bennett ... said"

Bennett, "Is the Novel Decaying?" *Cassell's Weekly*, March 28, 1923, p. 47

Supportive Source:

William Makepeace Thackeray, *The History of Pendennis*. (Orig. 1849-50)

Important Allusions:

(1) John Galsworthy

(2) Various H.G. Wells characters:

(a) Artie Kipps (in *Kipps* [1905])

(b) George Edgar Lewisham (in *Love and Mr. Lewisham* [1900])

(3) Bennett, *The Old Wives' Tale*. (Orig. 1908)

(4) Samuel Butler, *The Way of All Flesh*. (Orig. 1903)

Woolf reviewed this (2nd ed.) for *TLS*, June 26, 1919, p. 347.

(5) Various novels by Fyodor Dostoevskii [*sic*]:

(a) *Crime and Punishment*, trans. by Constance Garnett. Heinemann, 1914. (Orig. 1867)

(b) *The Idiot*, trans. by Constance Garnett. Heinemann, 1913. (Orig. 1882)

Passing Allusions:

Various characters:

(1) In Charles Dickens: Mr. Dick [Richard Babley], Mrs. Emma Micawber (in *David Copperfield*[1850]); Mr. Brooker (in *Nicholas Nickleby* [1839])

(2) In Dostoevsky: Rodion Romanovich Raskolnikov (in *Crime and Punishment*); Prince Lev Nicolaevich Mishkin (in *The Idiot*); Nikolay Vsevolodovich Stavrogin (in *The Possessed* [1871]); Alyosha [Alexsey Fyodorovich Karamazov] (in *The Brothers Karamazov* [1879])

MR. BENSON'S MEMORIES (1924)   C246.3

>   Obvious Source: Reading notes
>   #19
>   >   Arthur C. Benson, *Memories and Friends*. Murray,
>   >   1924.
>
>   Supportive Source:
>
>   >   "another of [Mr. Benson's] books"
>
>   >   Cannot locate
>
>   Important Allusion (mentioned by Benson):
>
>   >   Rupert Brooke
>
>   Passing Allusion (mentioned by Benson):
>
>   >   Henry James

- -

MR. CONRAD'S CRISIS (1918)   C102

>   Obvious Source:
>
>   >   Joseph Conrad, *Nostromo: A Tale of the Seaboard*.
>   >   Dent, 1918. (Orig. 1904)
>
>   Passing Allusion (mentioned by Conrad [in Preface]):
>
>   >   Conrad, *Typhoon*. (Orig. 1903)

- -

MR. CONRAD'S "YOUTH" (1917)   C86

>   Obvious Source:
>
>   >   Joseph Conrad, *Youth*, [w/"Author's Note"].
>   >   Dent, 1917. (Orig. 1902)
>
>   Supportive Source:
>
>   >   "Mr. Arnold Bennett recently protested"

Jacob Tonson [pseud. of Bennett], "The British
Academy of Letters," orig. in *New Age*, 7 (Aug.
18, 1910), 372-73; repr. in Bennett,*Books and
Persons*. Chatto and Windus, 1917.

Woolf reviewed this for *TLS*, July 5, 1917, p.
319.

Important Allusions:

Works by Conrad:

(1) Mentioned by Conrad (in "Author's Note"):

(a) *The Heart of Darkness*. (Orig. 1902)

(b) *The End of the Tether*. (Orig. 1902)

(2) *Chance*. (Orig. 1913)

(3) *Victory*. (Orig. 1915)

Passing Allusion:

Thomas Hardy

- -

MR. GLADSTONE'S DAUGHTER   C92

Obvious Source:

[Mary Gladstone Drew, *et al*.], *Some Hawarden Letters, 1878-1913*, arr. by Lisle March-Phillipps
and Bertram Christian. Nisbet, 1917.

Specific letters quoted from or paraphrased:

(1) Sir Mountstuart Grant Duff to Miss M. Gladstone, Aug. 16, 1884

(2) Sir Arthur Gordon to same, Jan. 27, 1882

(3) *Re* Bishop of London

(a) Same to same, Apr. 24, 1884

(b) James Stuart to same, Jan. 10, 1885

(4) *Re* poet's pension

Cannot locate

(5) From John Ruskin

    (a) "to his publisher"

        I.e., to George Allen, Jan. 18, 1878

    (b) "to Mrs. Drew [then still M. Gladstone]"

        Oct. 23, 1880

    (c) "his further vociferations"

        To Miss M. Gladstone, March 28 [29], 1882

(6) *Re* "anti-Froude society"

    Edward Burne Jones to same, Apr. 15, 1881

(7) *Re* "crusade" of newspaper owner William Thomas Stead

    (a) "discussed passionately"

        James Stuart to same, July 4, Sept. 30, and Nov. 22, 1885

    (b) "discussed ... gravely [by Alfred Lyttelton]"

        Cannot locate

Important Allusion:

    Ruskin, *Fors Clavigera*. (Orig. 1871-76)

Passing Allusions:

(1) Miscellaneous English writers: Benjamin Disraeli, Horace Walpole

(2) Mentioned by editor(s):

    James Anthony Froude, *Thomas Carlyle: A History of the First Forty Years of Life, 1795-1835*. 2 vol. Longman, Green, 1882.

(3) Various works mentioned in specific letters:

    (a) Henry George, *Progress and Poverty*. (Orig. 1879) Poss. ed.: Kegan Paul, 1882.

        (i) Edward Burne Jones to Miss M. Gladstone, July (?), 1883

(ii) James Stuart to same, Aug. 13 and
        Sept. 30, 1883

(b) W[ilhelmine] von Hillern, *The Vulture
    Maiden*. (Orig. 1875) Poss. ed.: Trans.
    by C. Bell and E.F. Poynter. Leipzig:
    B.Tauchnitz, 1876.

    H[enry] S[cott] Holland to same, n.d.,
    1883

(c) Mrs. [Mary Augusta] Humphry Ward, *Rob-
    ert Elsmere*. Smith and Elder, 1888.

    James Stuart to Mrs. Mary Drew, Aug.
    25, 1888

(d) George Meredith, *Diana of the Crossways*.
    3 vol. Chapman and Hall, 1885.

    (i) Henry Sidgwick to Miss M. Gladstone,
        n.d., 1885

    (ii) H[enry] S[cott] Holland to same,
         July (?), 1885

(e) Harriet Beecher Stowe, *The Minister's
    Wooing*. (Orig. 1859) Poss. ed.: Lon-
    don: N.p., 1869.

    Alfred Lyttelton to same, Sept. 28, 1884

(f) Henry James, "Madame de Mauves." (Orig.
    1874) Prob. ed.: James, Vol. 11 of "Col-
    lective Edition." Macmillan, 1883.

    H[enry] S[cott] Holland to same, n.d.,
    1883

(g) William James Dawson, *Redemption of Ed-
    ward Strachan*. Hodder and Stoughton,
    1891.

    Same to Mrs. Mary Drew, n.d. [1893?]

MR. GOSSE AND HIS FRIENDS (1919)   C168

Obvious Source:

Edmund Gosse, *Some Diversions of a Man of Letters.* Heinemann, 1919.

Important Allusions:

(1) "the letters of Edward FitzGerald"

E.g., *Letters and Literary Remains of Edward FitzGerald.* 7 vol. Macmillan, 1902-03.

This is listed in Holleyman; it belonged to Virginia.

(2) Miscellaneous writers (mentioned by Gosse): Charlotte Brontë, Lady Dorothy Nevill, Alfred Lord Tennyson, Paul Verlaine

Passing Allusions (mentioned by Gosse):

Miscellaneous English writers: Edward Bulwer-Lytton, Austin Dobson, John Locke, Joseph Warton, Thomas Warton

- -

MR.HENRY JAMES'S LATEST NOVEL (1905)   C06

Obvious Source: Reading notes
                                   B1a
        Henry James, *The Golden Bowl.* Methuen, 1905.

- -

MR. HOWELLS ON FORM (1918)   C131

Obvious Source:

Leonard Merrick, *The Actor Manager*, w/intro. by W[illiam] D[ean] Howells. Hodder and Stoughton, 1918.

Supportive Source:

"Gray ... has to write a letter"

Thomas Gray to the Rev. William Mason, March 28, 1767

2 poss. eds.:

(1) *The Poems of Mr. Gray. To Which Are Prefixed Memoirs of His Life and Writings by W[illiam] Mason.* 2nd ed. J. Dodsley, 1775.

This is listed in Holleyman.

(2) Thomas Gray, *Works of* ... , [ed. by John Mitford]. 5 vol. William Pickering, 1835-40. Vol. IV.

Vol. V is listed in Holleyman and Vols. I-IV in Holleyman Addendum; they belonged to Leslie Stephen.

Passing Allusions:

(1) Alexander Pope, *The Rape of the Lock.* (Orig. 1714)

(2) Miscellaneous English novelists: Jane Austen, Thomas Hardy, Thomas Love Peacock

(3) Marie Madeleine Motier, Countess de La Fayette, *La Princesse de Clèves.* (Orig. 1678)

- -

MR. SYMONS'S ESSAYS (1916)   C62

Obvious Source:

Arthur Symons, *Figures of Several Centuries.* Constable, 1916.

Specific essays quoted from:

(1) "the saying of Charles Lamb"; "love" should read "like"

"Charles Lamb." (Orig. 1905)

Cannot locate [in Lamb's works].

Quote 6 is also from here.

(2) Quote 2

"Coventry Patmore." (Orig. 1906)

Quote 10 (*re* Walt Whitman, *Leaves of Grass*, [1855]) is also from here.

(3) "as [Symons] says with ... truth" (quote 3)

"Walter Pater." (Orig. 1906)

Quote 9 (*re* Pater) is also from here.

(4) "his saying about Meredith" (quote 4)

"George Meredith as a Poet." (Orig. 1901)

(5) "This, too, is very true" (quote 5)

"John Donne." (Orig. 1899)

Quote 11 is also from here.

(7) "He can write of Ibsen" (quotes 7-8)

"Henrik Ibsen." (Orig. 1906)

Important Allusion (mentioned by Symons):

Algernon Charles Swinburne

Passing Allusions:

(1) Miscellaneous critics: Matthew Arnold, Samuel Taylor Coleridge, Charles Augustin Sainte-Beuve

(2) Miscellaneous writers: Thomas Carlyle, Fyodor Dostoevsky, Leo Tolstoy

- -

MR. YEATS (1928)   C301

Obvious Source:

William Butler Yeats, *The Tower*. Macmillan, 1928.

Specific poems quoted from:

(1) "The Tower." (Orig. 1926)

(2) "Nineteen-Nineteen." (Orig. 1919; "striped" should read "stupid," "lock" should read "locks")

(3) "Leda and the Swan." (Orig. 1923)

MRS. GRUNDY'S CRUCIFIX (1906)   C5.2

    Obvious Source: Reading notes
                                             B1a
        Vincent Brown, *Mrs. Grundy's Crucifix*. Hutchin-
        son, 1906.

- -

NANCY STAIR (1905)   See p. 178, KP

    Obvious Source: Reading notes
                                             B1a
        Elinor MacCartney Lane, *Nancy Stair*. Heine-
        mann, 1905.

    Passing Allusions:

        (1) Mentioned by Lane: Robert Burns

        (2) Marjorie Fleming

            Friend of Sir Walter Scott; also subject of
            John Brown, *Pet Marjorie: A Story of Child
            Life Fifty Years Ago*. (Orig. 1858)

- -

"THE NEW CRUSADE" (1917)   C95.1

    Obvious Source:

        John Drinkwater, *Prose Papers*. Elkin Mathew,
        1917.

        (1) Specific essays quoted from:

            (a) Paragraph 1

                "Frederick Tennyson"

                Quote, paragraph 3, is also from here;
                there should be ellipses after "tech-
                nique"

            (b) Paragraph 2

                (i) "he writes in his dedication"
                    (first quote)

(ii) Quotes 2-4

"The Value of Poetry in Education"

(iii) "he says"

Paraphrase of "Poetry and Conduct"

(2) Specific essay mentioned but not quoted from:

"Rupert Brooke"

Passing Allusion (mentioned by Drinkwater):

William Shakespeare

- -

THE NEW RELIGION (1907)   C6.1

Obvious Source:

Maarten Maartens, *The New Religion*. Methuen, 1907.

- -

NEXT-DOOR NEIGHBOURS (1905)   C03

Obvious Source:

W. Pett Ridge, *Next-Door Neighbours*. Hodder and Stoughton, 1905.

- -

A NINETEENTH-CENTURY CRITIC (1906)   C3.1

Obvious Source:

Canon [Alfred] Ainger, *Lectures and Essays*, w/intro. by H.C. Beeching. 2 vol. Macmillan, 1906.

Specific essays quoted from:

(1) "The Ethical Element in Shakespeare." Vol. I.

    (a) "a saying of Coventry Patmore"

        "Poetical Integrity," in Patmore, *Principle in Art.* (Orig. 1889)

    (b) "the lines" (quoted also by Patmore)

        William Wordsworth, "Ode. Intimations of Immortality...." (Orig. 1807) Ll. 206-07.

    (c) Quotes 2-4 are also from here.

(2) Quotes 5-9

    (a) "The Death of Tennyson." Vol. II.

    (b) "The Art of Conversation" (2 quotes). Vol. II.

    (c) "The Secret of Charm in Literature" (2 quotes). Vol. II; "that is" should be in brackets.

        Ainger in this essay makes the same point about Patmore and quotes the same lines from Wordsworth as he does in (1) above.

Important Allusions (mentioned by Ainger):

    Miscellaneous English writers: Lord Byron (mentioned also by Patmore), Stephen Phillips

Passing Allusions (mentioned by Ainger):

    Miscellaneous English poets: John Keats, Christopher Marlowe, Percy Bysshe Shelley

- -

THE NOVELS OF GEORGE GISSING (1912)   C48

    Stated Impulse:

        Works by Gissing (new ed.; Sidgwick and Jackson, 1911)

 (1) *The Odd Women.* (Orig. 1893)

 (2) *Eve's Ransom.* (Orig. 1895)

 (3) *The Whirlpool.* (Orig. 1897)

 (4) *The Unclassed.* (Orig. 1884)

 (5) *The Emancipated.* (Orig. 1890)

 (6) *In the Year of Jubilee.* (Orig. 1894)

 (7) *Denzil Quarrier.* (Orig. 1892)

 (8) *Human Odds and Ends.* (Orig. 1898)

Inferred Sources:

 Other works by Gissing:

 (1) *Born in Exile.* (Orig. 1892)

 (2) *New Grub Street.* (Orig. 1891)

 (3) *The Nether World.* (Orig. 1889)

 (4) *Demos.* (Orig. 1886)

  Quote, next-to-last paragraph, is from here.

Supportive Source:

 "An interesting letter ... was printed the other day"

 Gissing to Edward Clodd, Nov. 7, 1899

 Cannot locate (repr. later in *Letters to Edward Clodd from George Gissing.* [T.J. Wise, 1914])

Passing Allusions:

 (1) Miscellaneous writers: Charles Dickens, Euripides (mentioned by Gissing), Elizabeth Gaskell

 (2) Various characters: Jane Eyre; Uncle Toby (in Laurence Sterne, *Tristram Shandy* [1759-67])

 (3) George Meredith, *Evan Harrington.* (Orig. 1861)

OLD AND YOUNG (1916)   C60

    Obvious Source:

        Stephen Paget, *I Sometimes Think*.   Macmillan,
        1916.

        (1) Specific quotes from:

            (a) "his own contention"

            In Preface

            (b) "he says"; "he bids us"; "he adds";
                "this essay" (quotes 2-5)

            "The World, Myself, and Thee"

        (2) Essays mentioned but not quoted from:

            (a) "Moving Pictures"

            (b) "Handwritings"

            (c) "The Beauty of Words"

- -

AN OLD NOVEL (1920)   C193

    Obvious Source:

        Ashford Owen [pseud. of Anna Charlotte Ogle], *A
        Lost Love*.   New ed., [with "Personal Note" by
        Frances M. Charlton].   Murray, 1920.   (Orig.
        1855)

    Important Allusion:

        Mentioned by Owen and Charlton: Sir Henry Taylor

- -

ON NOT KNOWING FRENCH (1929)   C308

    Inferred Source (mentioned in   Reading notes
                fifth paragraph):   #13

        André Maurois, *Climats*.   Paris: Bernard Grasset,
        1928.

Important Allusions:

>   (1) Miscellaneous writers: Joseph Conrad, Henry
>   James, Duc de Saint Simon
>
>   (2) "M. Maurois' lives of [Percy Bysshe] Shelley
>   and [Benjamin] Disraeli"
>
>   (a) *Ariel.* (Orig. 1923)
>
>   (b) *La vie de Disraëli.* (Orig. 1927)

Passing Allusions:

>   (1) Miscellaneous writers: Lord Byron, Prosper
>   Mérimée, Samuel Pepys, Edgar Allan Poe
>
>   (2) Odile Malet (character in *Climats* [see
>   above])

- -

ON SOME OF THE OLD ACTORS (1919)   C154

Obvious Source:

>   Joseph Francis Daly, *The Life of Augustin Daly.*
>   Macmillan, 1919.

Passing Allusions (mentioned by J. Daly):

>   (1) Miscellaneous English playwrights: William
>   Shakespeare, William Wycherley
>
>   (2) Various characters: Meg Merrilies (in Sir
>   Walter Scott, *Guy Mannering* [1815]); Emilia
>   (in Shakespeare, *Othello* [publ. 1622])
>
>   (3) "Knight's Shakespeare"
>
>   *The Plays of Shakespeare*, w/notes by Charles
>   Knight. 6 vol. Virtue, [1906-10].
>
>   (4) Henry Hamilton and Cecil Raleigh, *The Great
>   Ruby*. (Orig. 1898)

ON THE STAGE (1928)   C301.4

    Obvious Source:

        George Arliss, *On the Stage: an Autobiography.*
        Murry, 1928.

- -

PARADISE IN PICCADILLY (1926)   C272.1

    Obvious Source:

        Harry Furniss, *Paradise in Piccadilly.*   Bodley
        Head, 1925.

    Important Allusion (mentioned by Furniss):

        Thomas Babington Macaulay

    Passing Allusion (mentioned by Furniss):

        George Gordon, Lord Byron

- -

PARODIES (1917)   C68

    Obvious Source:

        J[ohn] C[ollings] Squire, *Tricks of the Trade.*
        Martin Secker, 1917.

    Important Allusions (mentioned by Squire):

        (1) Miscellaneous British writers: Lord Byron,
            W[illiam] H[enry] Davies, Thomas Gray, Sir
            Henry Newbolt, Alexander Pope, George Ber-
            nard Shaw, H[erbert] G[eorge] Wells

        (2) Edgar Lee Masters, *Spoon River Anthology.*
            (Orig. 1915)

        (3) Works by Alfred Lord Tennyson:

            (a) "The Passing of Arthur." (Orig. 1869)

            (b) "Break, Break, Break." (Orig. 1842)

    Passing Allusion (mentioned by Squire):

        Hilaire Belloc

PAST AND PRESENT AT THE ENGLISH LAKES (1916)   C52.1

Obvious Source:

Canon [Hardwicke Drummond] Rawnsley, *Past and Present at the English Lakes*. Glasgow: MacLehose, 1916.

Specific essays mentioned:

(1) "Crossing the Sands"

(2) "the most interesting paper in the book"

"The Story of Gough and His Dog"

"versions of the same story" (mentioned by Rawnsley):

(a) "by a journalist"

Identity uncertain

(b) "by [Sir Walter] Scott"

"Helvellyn." (Orig. 1805)

(c) "by [William] Wordsworth"

"Fidelity." (Orig. 1807)

(d) "by [Thomas] DeQuincey"

"Early Memorials of Grasmere." (Orig. 1839)

Passing Allusion (mentioned by Rawnsley):

Samuel Taylor Coleridge

- -

"PATTLEDOM" (1925)   C265.1

Obvious Source:

Lady [Laura] Troubridge, *Memories and Reflections*. Heinemann, 1925.

Passing Allusions:

Miscellaneous English writers:

(a) George Meredith

(b) Mentioned by Troubridge: Sir Henry Tay-
    lor, Alfred Lord Tennyson

- -

PEGGY (1924)   C256.2

Obvious Source:

Peggy Webling, *Peggy: The Story of One Score
Years and Ten.* Hutchinson, 1924.

Important Allusion (mentioned by Webling):

(1) Miscellaneous British writers: Lord Byron,
    John Ruskin, Oscar Wilde

(2) Samuel Johnson, *A Dicionary of the English
    Language.* (Orig. 1755)

- -

THE PERFECT LANGUAGE (1917)   C75

Obvious Source:

The Greek Anthology, trans. by W[illiam] R. Pa-
ton. Loeb Classical Library ed. Heinemann,
[1916-18]. (Orig. 6th cent. B.C.-6th cent. A.D.)
Vol. II, 1917.

Specific quotes from (all first cent. B.C.):

(1) "We have only to open this volume ... at
    hazard"

    Simonides, "Sepulchral Epigram 254A."

(2) "Let us turn the page"

    Theodoridas, "Sepulchral Epigram 282."

(3) "or ... "

    (a) Simonides, "Sepulchral Epigram 253."

    (b) Meleager, "Sepulchral Epigram 476."

Supportive Sources:

> (1) William Shakespeare, *The Winter's Tale*,
>   IV:4:115-17. (Orig. publ. 1623)
>
>   First quote is from here.
>
> (2) *Select Epigrams from the Greek Anthology*,
>   ed. and trans. by J[ohn] W[illiam] MacKail.
>   New ed. Longmans, Green, 1907.
>
>   This is listed in Holleyman.
>
>   Last quote is from here:
>
>   Meleager, "Love in Spring" ([Amatory Epi-
>   gram]; orig. first cent. B.C.)

Passing Allusions:

> Miscellaneous Greek writers: Aeschylus, Homer,
> Sophocles

- -

PHILIP SIDNEY (1907)   C5.12

Obvious Source:

> Sir Fulke Greville, *Life of Sir Philip Sidney*,
> w/intro. by Nowell Smith. Tudor and Stuart Li-
> brary ser. Oxford: Clarendon, 1907. (Orig.
> 1652)

Supportive Source:

> "says Lamb"
>
> Charles Lamb, Note to extract from Sir Fulke
> Greville, *Mustapha* [1609), in Lamb, *Specimens of
> English Dramatics Poets....* (Orig. 1808) Poss.
> ed.: *The Works of Charles and Mary Lamb*, ed. by
> E.V. Lucas. 7 vol. Methuen, 1903-05. Vol. IV.

Important Allusion (mentioned by Greville):

> Sidney, *The Countess of Pembroke's Arcadia*. (Or-
> ig. 1593)

Passing Allusions:

> (1) Don Quixote

    (2) Mentioned by Greville:

        (a) Sidney, *A Defence of Poesie.* (Orig.
            1595)

        (b) Edmund Spenser

- -

PICTURES AND PORTRAITS (1920)   C182

    Obvious Source:

        Edmund X. Kapp, *Personalities. Twenty-Four
        Drawings.* Secker, 1919.

    Important Allusion (mentioned by Kapp):

        George Bernard Shaw

    Passing Allusions:

        Various characters: Mrs. Grundy (in Thomas Mor-
        ton, *Speed the Plough* [1800]), Don Quixote

- -

A PLAYER UNDER THREE REIGNS (1925)   C262.2

    Obvious Source: Reading notes
                                       B2o
        Sir Johnston Forbes Robertson, *A Player Under
        Three Reigns.* Fisher Unwin, 1925.

    Passing Allusions:

        (1) Mentioned by Robertson:

            (a) Miscellaneous English poets: Dante Ga-
                briel Rossetti, William Shakespeare, Al-
                gernon Charles Swinburne

            (b) Samuel Butler, *Erewhon.* (Orig. 1872)

        (2) Hamlet

PLAYS ... (1928)   C305.1

   Supportive Sources:

      (1) Igor Stravinsky, *The Tale of a Soldier*.
          (Orig. 1918)

      (2) William Shakespeare, *A Lover's Complaint*.
          (Orig. 1609)

- -

THE POEMS ... OF ... LORD HERBERT OF CHERBURY (1924)   C242.

   Obvious Source:

      Edward, Lord Herbert of Cherbury, *The Poems, English and Latin, of* ... , ed. by G.C. Moore Smith.
      Oxford: Clarendon, 1923.

   Important Allusion:

      "the famous autobiography"

      Edward, Lord Herbert of Cherbury, *The Life of* ...
      (Orig. publ. 1764; Lord Herbert's dates were
      1583-1648)

   Passing Allusion (mentioned by Smith):

      George Herbert

- -

THE POETIC DRAMA (1906)   C3.9

   Obvious Sources: Reading notes
                                           B1a
      (1) Arthur Dillon, *King William I*.   Elkin Mathews, 1905.

      (2) Spencer Moore, *Aurelian*. Longmans Green,
          1905.

      (3) Archibald Douglas Fox, *Sir Thomas More*.
          Constable, 1905.

      (4) Alexandra Von Herder, *The Little Mermaid*.
          Elkin Mathews, 1906.

(5) Arthur Upson, *The City*. New York: Macmillan, 1906.

(6) Paul Hookham, *Plays and Poems*. Kegan Paul, 1906.

(7) Rosalind Travers, *The Two Arcadias*. Brimley Johnson, 1905.

Passing Allusions:

    (1) Euripides

    (2) Various works:

        (a) Matthew Arnold, "The Forsaken Merman." (Orig. 1849)

        (b) "Lafontaine's Fables"

            Jean de La Fontaine, *Fables Choisies*. (Orig. 1668; first Engl. trans. 1806)

- -

POETS' LETTERS (1906)   C4

Obvious Sources: Reading notes
                                        B1a
    (1) Percy Lubbock, *Elizabeth Barrett Browning in Her Letters*. Smith, Elder, 1906.

        Specific letters quoted from:

        (a) Paragraph 3

            Elizabeth Barrett to Robert Browning, March 20, 1845

        (b) Paragraph 4

            Elizabeth Barrett Browning to John Ruskin, June 2, 1855; "called" should read "thought"

        (c) Paragraph 5

            Elizabeth Barrett to Mrs. James Martin, Sept. 10, 1844; "success" should read "successes"

(2) *Robert Browning and Alfred Domett*, ed. by
     Frederic G. Kenyon. Smith, Elder, 1906.

     Specific letters quoted from (paragraph 6):

     (a) From Robert Browning

              (i) To Isabella Blagden, March 30,
                  1872

             (ii) To Domett, Oct. 9, 1843; "the ship"
                  should read "a ship"

            (iii) To same, July 31, 1844; there
                  should be ellipses before "and"

             (iv) To same, Oct. 9, 1843

              (v) To same, May 22, 1842

             (vi) To same, March 5, 1843

     (b) Joseph Arnould to Domett, n.d. [Sept.
         1843(?)]; there should be ellipses be-
         tween "I" and "believe"

Passing Allusions (mentioned by Arnould):

     (1) Robert Browning, *Paracelsus*. (Orig. 1835)

     (2) William Shakespeare

- -

PORTRAITS OF PLACES (1906)   See p. 179, #9
                                        (bottom), KP
     Obvious Source:

     Henry James, *Portraits of Places*. (Orig. 1883)
     Prob. ed.: Macmillan, 1906.

     Specific essay quoted from:

     "In Warwickshire"; orig. in *The Galaxy*, 24 (Nov.
     1877), 603-11.

     Quotes, paragraph 4, are from here; "eye" should
     read "eyes"; there should be ellipses between
     "other" and "He," "dressed" and "'I,'" and
     "interlocutress" and "and"

Important Allusion (mentioned by James):

William Shakespeare

Passing Allusion (mentioned by James):

Mrs. [Nell] Quickly (character in Shakespeare,
Henry IV, Part 1[1598]; *Henry IV, Part 2* [1600];
The Merry Wives of Windsor [1602]; *Henry V*
[1600]

- -

A POSITIVIST (1919)   C158

Obvious Source:

Frederic Harrison, *Obiter Scripta, 1918*.   Chapman and Hall, 1919.

Important Allusion (mentioned by Harrison):

"'an article in the very first number of the
Fortnightly'" (periodical, 1865-1954)

F. Harrison, "The Iron-Masters' Trade Union,"
Fortnightly, 1 (May 15, 1865), 96ff.

Passing Allusions (mentioned by Harrison):

(1) Miscellaneous writers: Aeschylus, Jane Aus-
ten, Walter Bagehot, George Eliot [pseud. of
Mary Ann Evans], Edward Augustus Freeman,
Thomas Hardy, Horace, Thomas Huxley, William
E. Hartpole Lecky, George Henry Lewes, George
Meredith, John Morley, Walter Pater, Mark
Pattison, Rabelais, Sir Walter Scott, Soph-
ocles, Herbert Spencer, Leslie Stephen,
Algernon Charles Swinburne, Anthony Trollope,
Virgil

(2) Various works:

(a) Eliot Warburton, *The Crescent and the
Cross*. (Orig. 1845)

(b) Alexander William Kinglake, *Eothen*.
(Orig. 1845)

A PRACTICAL UTOPIA (1918)   C118

    Oliver Onions, *The New Moon*. Hodder and Stoughton,
    1918.

- -

PREFERENCES (1928)   C300

    Supportive Sources:

        (1) "Jean-Aubry's life of Conrad"

            G. Jean Aubry, *Joseph Conrad. Life and Let-
            ters*. 2 vol. William Heinemann, 1927.

        (2) Gertrude Bell, *The Letters of* ... , sel. and
            ed. by Lady [Florence] Bell. 2 vol. Ernest
            Benn, 1927.

        (3) George Sturt, *A Small Boy in the Sixties*.
            Cambridge: Univ. Pr., 1927.

        (4) Thomas Lister, Baron Ribblesdale, *Impressions
            and Memories*, w/pref. by his daughter, Lady
            Wilson. Cassell, 1927.

        (5) Anthony Hope, *Memories and Notes*. Hutchin-
            son, 1927.

            She reviewed this for *Nation and Athenaeum*,
            Feb. 11, 1928, p. 728. (See "Memories and
            Notes.")

        (6) Laurence J.L. Dundas, *The Life of Lord Cur-
            zon*. 3 vol. Ernest Benn, 1928. Vol. I.

        (7) Lady Anne Winchilsea, *Poems* ... *1661-1720*,
            sel. by John Middleton Murry. Jonathan Cape,
            1928.

        (8) William Butler Yeats, *The Tower*. Macmillan,
            1928.

            She reviewed this for *Nation and Athenaeum*,
            Apr. 21, 1928, p. 81. ("See Mr. Yeats.")

    Important Allusion:

        Marcel Proust, *A la Recherche du Temps Perdu*.
        (Orig. 1914-27)

Passing Allusions:

> (1) Elizabeth Bowen, *The Hotel*. Constable, 1927.
>
> (2) Thornton Wilder, *The Bridge of San Luis Rey*. Longmans, 1927.
>
> (3) Julien Green, *Avarice House*, trans. by M.A. Best. New York and London: Harper, 1927.

- -

A PRINCE OF PROSE (1921)   C216

Obvious Source:

> Joseph Conrad, *Notes on Life and Letters*. Dent, 1921.
>
> Specific quotes from:
>
> (1) "Author's Note"
>
> > Quote, paragraph 2, is from here; also paragraph 3, quotes 1-2.
>
> (2) "his own phrase about Anatole France"
>
> > "'Crainquebille.'" (Orig. 1904)
> >
> > Paraphrase, paragraph 3, is from here; also paragraph 5, quote 3.
>
> (3) "he says of [Ivan] Turgenev"
>
> > "Turgenev." (Orig. 1917)
> >
> > Paragraph 3, quotes 3-4, are from here.
>
> (4) "Henry James." (Orig. 1905)
>
> > Quote, paragraph 4, and paragraph 5, first quote, are from here.
>
> (5) "Guy de Maupassant." (Orig. 1904)
>
> > Paragraph 5, quotes 2 and 4, are from here.
>
> (6) Paragraph 5, quote 5:
>
> > "Books." (Orig. 1905)

(7) "Alphonse Daudet." (Orig. 1898)

All quotes, paragraph 6, are from here.

Supportive Source:

George Conrad, *The Rescue*. Dent, 1920.

She reviewed this for *TLS* , July 1, 1920, p. 419. (See "A Disillusioned Romantic.")

Passing Allusions:

Miscellaneous writers: Jane Austen, John Donne, Jean Baptiste Poquelin Moliere, Jean Baptiste Racine

- -

THE PRIVATE PAPERS OF HENRY RYECROFT (1907)   C5.8

Obvious Source: Reading notes
                                          B1a
George Gissing, *The Private Papers of Henry Rye-croft*. Constable, 1903.

Specific quote from (paragraph 3):

William Shakespeare, *Henry IV, Part 2*: III:ii: 228. (Orig. 1600)

Passing Allusion (mentioned by Gissing):

Laurence Sterne, *Tristram Shandy*. (Orig. 1759-67)

- -

PURE ENGLISH (1920)   C199

Obvious Source:

[William Stevenson(?)], *Gammer Gurton's Needle*, ed. by H.F.B. Brett-Smith. Oxford: Blackwell, 1920. (Orig. 1575)

QUEEN ALEXANDRA THE WELL-BELOVED (1926)   C271.1

    Obvious Source:

        Elizabeth Villiers, *Queen Alexandra the Well-
        Beloved.* Stanley Paul, 1925.

- -

RACHEL (1911)   C47

    Obvious Source:

        Francis Gribble, *Rachel: Her Stage Life and Her
        Real Life.* Chapman and Hall, 1911.

        Specific quotes from:

        (1) Paragraph 4

            (a) "[Rachel] cried"; "have lived" should
                read "have to live"

                Cannot locate

            (b) "[Rachel]said"

                Ernest Legouvé, *Soixante Ans de Souve-
                nirs.* 2 vol. Paris: N.p., 1886-87.

                Apparently oral tradition

        (2) Paragraph 5

            Charlotte Brontë, *Villette.* (Orig. 1853)

    Passing Allusion (mentioned by Gribble):

        Alfred de Musset

- -

THE READER (1941; publ. in 1979)   Not in KP; ed.
                              by Brenda Silver*

    Inferred Source:

                             Reading notes
        "the pages of Lady Anne   #16 and B2c
        Cliffords [*sic*] diary"

        (See "Anon.")+

This is listed in the reading notes (#16).

Specific quotes from (pp. 427-28):

(1) First quote

1603 [reminiscence]

(2) Quote 2

Jan. [18], 1617

(3) Quote 3

March [4], 1619; "and indiscreet" should read "an indiscreet"

(4) Quote 5

Jan. [5], 1617

(5) Quote 6

Jan. [6], 1617

Supportive Sources:

(1) George C. Williamson, *Lady Anne Clifford....* Kendal: Titus Wilson, 1922.+

Quote 4, p. 427, is from here: Lady Anne to the Countess Dowager of Kent, Jan. 6, 1649; in the original, "pitiable" read "pitable"

(2) Robert Burton, *The Anatomy of Melancholy*, ed. by A.R. Shilleto. 3 vol. Bell, 1893. (Orig. 1621)

This is indicated by the reading notes (#16)+ and is listed in Holleyman Addendum; it belonged to Leonard.

(3) "Morgann could say"

Maurice Morgann, *An Essay on the Dramatic Character of Sir John Falstaff.* (Orig. 1777)+ Prob. ed.: Ed. by William Arthur Gill. Oxford Library ed. Frowde, 1912.

This is listed in Holleyman.

Important Allusion (mentioned by Lady Clifford):

Geoffrey Chaucer

Passing Allusions:

> (1) Mentioned by Lady Clifford:
>
>> *The Mad Lover*. [Play seen at court Jan. 5, 1617]
>>
>> Cannot locate.
>
> (2) Miscellaneous 16th-century English writers: Ben Jonson, William Shakespeare, Philip Sidney

* See starred note for "Anon."

- -

REAL LETTERS (1919)   C173

Obvious Source:

> Emily Eden, *Miss Eden's Letters*, ed. by Violet Dickinson. Macmillan, 1919.

Specific quotes from:

> (1) "We will let Miss Eden ... speak"
>
>> Eden to Eleanor, Lady Buckinghamshire, Oct. 7, [1819]
>
> (2) "Pamela now takes up the pen"
>
>> Pamela, Lady Campbell, to Eden, March 3, 1821
>
> (3) "wrote Pamela"; "she added"
>
>> Same to same, Feb. 28, 1821
>
> (4) "Miss Eden ... was ... pleased"
>
>> Same to same, Aug. 16, 1836
>
> (5) *Re* Prime Minister
>
>> V. Dickinson, connecting note (p. 114)
>
> (6) "the family version of [Lady Sarah's] vagaries"
>
>> Eden to Theresa Villiers, [Nov. (?)], 1827
>
> (7) *Re* Lady Sarah and stables
>
>> Same to same, Dec. 15, 1826

(8) *Re* Mrs. Elton (character in Jane Austen, *Emma* [1816])

Same to same, n.d. [1825]

(9) *Re* Mr. Collins (character in Austen, *Pride and Prejudice* [1813])

Same to same, [Aug. or Sept. (?)], 1826

Important Allusions (mentioned by Dickinson):

Novels by Eden

(1) *The Semi-Detached House*. (Orig. 1859)

(2) *The Semi-Attached Couple*. (Orig. 1860)

Passing Allusion (mentioned by Eden):

James Boswell

- -

REBELS AND REFORMERS (1917)   C94

Obvious Source:

Arthur and Dorothea Ponsonby, *Rebels and Reformers*. Allen and Unwin, 1917.

Specific quote from:

"cry ... from ... Countess Tolstoy"

Countess Sophia Andreyevna Tolstaya to Tanya Be(h)rs Kuzminskaya, March (?), 1883

Important Allusion (mentioned by Ponsonbys):

Leo Tolstoy

Passing Allusions:

Miscellaneous writers

(1) William Shakespeare

(2) Mentioned by Ponsonbys: Hans Andersen, Miguel de Cervantes Saavedra, François Marie Arouet de Voltaire

RECENT PAINTINGS BY VANESSA BELL (1930)   B10

     Passing Allusions:

          Miscellaneous English novelists: Charles Dick-
          ens, William Makepeace Thackeray

- -

RECENT PAINTINGS BY VANESSA BELL (1934)   B11.1

     Supportive Source:

          John Keats to Benjamin Robert Haydon, Apr. 8,
          1818

          Prob. ed.: Keats, *Letters of* ... , ed. by Sid-
          ney Colvin. [Rev. ed.] Macmillan, 1918. (Orig.
          1891)

          This is listed in Holleyman.

- -

REMINISCENCES OF MRS. COMYNS CARR (1926)   C272.2

     Obvious Source:

          Mrs. [Alice] Comyns Carr, *Reminiscences of* ... ,
          ed. by Eve Adam. Hutchinson, [1925].

     Passing Allusions (mentioned by Carr):

          Miscellaneous writers: Henry James, George Mere-
          dith, Oscar Wilde

- -

RESTORATION COMEDY (1924)   C258

     Obvious Sources: Reading notes
                                        B2o
          (1) Bonamy Dobrée, *Restoration Comedy, 1660-1720.*
              Oxford: Clarendon, 1924.

          (2) Edmund Gosse, *The Life of William Congreve.*
              Rev. and enl. ed. Heinemann, 1924. (Orig.
              1888)

Important Allusions (mentioned by Dobrée):

    (1) Plays by William Wycherley:

        (a) *The Country Wife.* (Orig. 1675)

        (b) *The Plain Dealer.* (Orig. 1677)

    (2) Jean Baptiste Poquelin Molière, *Le Misan-thrope.* (Orig. 1666)

Passing Allusions (mentioned by Dobrée):

    (1) Alceste (character in *Le Misanthrope*)

    (2) Miscellaneous Restoration playwrights: John Dryden, Sir George Etherege, George Farquhar, Thomas Shadwell, Sir John Vanbrugh

- -

RICHARD HAKLUYT (1924)   C255.3

    Obvious Source: Reading notes
                                    B2o
        Foster Watson, *Richard Hakluyt.* Pioneers of
        Progress ser. Sheldon, 1924.

    Specific quotes from:

    (1) Hakluyt, *Discourse Concerning Western Plant-ing.* (Orig. publ. 1877)

        Quotes 1 and 3 are from here; there should be ellipses between "people" and "forced."

    (2) Hakluyt, Dedication to Sir Walter Raleigh, in René de Laudonnière, *A Notable Historie Containing Four Voyages Made by Certayne French Captaynes unto Florida*, trans. by Hakluyt. T. Dawson, 1587. (Orig. 1586)

        Quote 2 is from here.

    Important Allusion (mentioned by Watson):

        "the great 'Navigations'"

        [Richard Hakluyt, ed.], *Hakluyt's Collection of the Early Voyages, Travels, and Discoveries of the English Nation.* (Orig. 1598-1600)

Passing Allusion:

    William Shakespeare

- -

ROBERT SMITH SURTEES (1924)   C246.6

    Obvious Source: Reading notes
                                          #19
        Robert Smith Surtees and E.D. Cuming, *Robert Smith
        Surtees (Creator of "Jorrocks"), 1803-1864.*
        Edinburgh: Blackwood, 1924.

    Important Allusions (mentioned by Surtees):

        (1) *New Sporting Magazine* (periodical, 1831-70)

        (2) John Jorrocks (character in Surtees, begin-
            ning with *Jorrocks's Jaunts and Jollities*
            [1838])

- -

ROMANCE (1917)   C63

    Obvious Source:

        Sir Walter [Alexander] Raleigh, *Romance.* Prince-
        ton, N.J.: Princeton U. Pr., 1916.

    Supportive Source:

        3rd quote from end

        William Wordsworth, "Elegaic Stanzas, Suggested
        by a Picture of Peele Castle." (Orig. 1805)
        L. 54.

    Important Allusions (mentioned by Raleigh):

        (1) Sir Walter Scott

        (2) "Ossian"

            Gaelic pseudonym of James Macpherson (1736-
            96), poet

Passing Allusions:

    (1) Mentioned by Raleigh

        (a) Miscellaneous writers: John Dryden,
            Henry Fielding, Alexander Pope, Virgil

        (b) Samuel Taylor Coleridge, *Kubla Khan*.
            (Orig. publ. 1816)

    (2) John Keats, "Ode to a Nightingale." (Orig.
        1819)

- -

ROMANCE AND THE NINETIES (1926)   C274.2

Obvious Source:

    Richard le Gallienne, *The Romantic 'Nineties*.
    Putnam, 1926.

Important Allusions (mentioned by le Gallienne):

    Miscellaneous English writers: Walter Pater,
    Algernon Charles Swinburne

Passing Allusions:

    Miscellaneous British writers

    (1) Mentioned by le Gallienne: John Davidson,
        Ernest Dowson, Rudyard Kipling, Arthur Sy-
        mons, Oscar Wilde, William Butler Yeats

    (2) Arnold Bennett, H[erbert] G[eorge] Wells

- -

ROSE OF LONE FARM (1905)   C2.01

Obvious Source: Reading notes
                                        B1a
    Eleanor G. Hayden, *Rose of Lone Farm*. Smith,
    Elder, 1905.

THE RUSSIAN VIEW (1918)   C136

   Obvious Source:

      Elena Militsina and Mikhail Saltikov, *The Village
      Priest, and Other Stories*, trans. by Beatrix
      L. Tollemache, w/intro. by C. Hagberg Wright.
      Fisher Unwin, 1918.

      Specific stories quoted from:

      (1) Saltikov, "Konyaga."

      (2) Militsina, "The Village Priest."

         Quote *re* "the feeble-minded" is also from
         here.

   Supportive Source:

      "one of Mr. Galsworthy's latest stories"

      John Galsworthy, "The First and the Last" (orig.
      1915); repr. in Galsworthy, *Five Tales*. William
      Heinemann, 1918.

- -

THE SAD YEARS (1918)   C119

   Obvious Source:

      Dora Sigerson, *The Sad Years*. Constable, 1918.

      Specific quotes from:

      (1) "writes Katharine Tynan"

         "Dora Sigerson. A Tribute and Some Memories";
         orig. in *The Observer*, Jan. 13, 1918; repr.
         in *The Sad Years*.

      (2) Sigerson, "I Saw Children Playing."

SAINT SAMUEL OF FLEET STREET (1925)   C269.1

Obvious Sources:

(1) James Boswell, *The Life of Samuel Johnson*,
    ed. by Arnold Glover, w/intro. by Austin Dob-
    son. 3 vol. Dent, 1925. (Orig. 1791)

(2) James Boswell, *The Life of Samuel Johnson*, ed.
    by Roger Ingpen. 2 vol. Bath: Bayntun,
    1925.

    Story of cabman is from here: quoted by
    Ingpen from John Cann Bailey, *Dr. Johnson
    and His Circle*. Williams and Norgate,
    [1913].

(3) James Boswell, *Boswell's Life of Johnson*,
    abr. and ed. by F.H. Pritchard. Harrap,
    1925.

Supportive Sources:

(1) "Canon [Alfred] Ainger called"

    Cannot locate

(2) Johnson, "Life of [John] Milton," in *The
    Lives of the Most Eminent English Poets*....
    (Orig. 1779-81)

    2 poss. eds.:

    (a) Chandos Classics ser. Frederick Warne,
        n.d. [1872?].

        This is listed in Holleyman; it belonged
        to Leslie Stephen.

    (b) ... *With a Sketch of the Author's Life
        by Sir Walter Scott*. F. Warne, n.d.

        This is listed in Holleyman Addendum; it
        belonged to Virginia.

Important Allusion:

    Charles Lamb

Passing Allusions:

(1) Works by Johnson (mentioned by Boswell)

    (a) *Rasselas*. (Orig. 1759 as *The Prince of
        Abissinia*)

(b) *The Rambler* (periodical, 1750-51)

(c) "The Vanity of Human Wishes." (Orig. 1749)

(d) "*Tour to the Hebrides*" [*sic*; i.e., *A Journey to the Western Islands of Scotland*]. (Orig. 1775)

(2) Miscellaneous writers: Sir Thomas Browne, William Congreve, Michel Eyquem de Montaigne, Samuel Pepys, Alexander Pope, William Shakespeare, Jonathan Swift, William Wycherley

- -

THE SCHOLAR'S DAUGHTER (1906)   C3.4

    Obvious Source: Reading notes
                                         B1a
        Beatrice Harraden, *The Scholar's Daughter.* Methuen, 1906.

- -

THE SCHOOLROOM FLOOR (1924)   C255

    Obvious Source:

        Mary MacCarthy, *A Nineteenth Century Childhood.* Heinemann, 1924.

    Passing Allusions (mentioned by MacCarthy):

        Miscellaneous writers: Robert Browning, Henry James, Charles Augustin Sainte-Beuve, Alfred Lord Tennyson

- -

SCOTTISH WOMEN (1908)   C16

    Obvious Source:

        Harry Graham, *A Group of Scottish Women.* Methuen, 1908.

Specific quote from:

"as Lady Anne Barnard [b. Lindsay] ... said"

Barnard to Sir Walter Scott, July 8, 1823; repr. in *Auld Robin Gray: A Ballad* ... Edinburgh: James Ballantyne, 1825. (Orig. 1772)

Passing Allusions (mentioned by Graham):

Miscellaneous British writers: John Gay, Isobel Pagan, Jonathan Swift

- -

SCOTT'S CHARACTER (1921)   C219

Obvious Source:

Archibald Stalker, *The Intimate Life of Sir Walter Scott*. Edinburgh: A. and C. Black, 1921.

Specific quote from:

"when the husband writes"

Scott to Lady Anne Jane Abercorn, Jan. 21, 1810

Supportive Sources:

(1) *Re* "The Duke of Buccleugh [*sic*; i.e., Buccleuch]" and "the 'old Knights of Branxholm'"

Cannot locate

[A reference book on Scottish clans shows David Scott of Branxholm as an ancestor of Buccleuch (and a collateral cousin of Sir Walter himself).]

(2) J[ohn] G[ibson] Lockhart, *Memoirs of the Life of Scott*. (Orig. 1837-38) Prob. ed.: 10 vol. Edinburgh: A. and C. Black, 1882.

This is listed in Holleyman; it belonged to Virginia.

Quotes *re* Mrs. [Harriot] Coutts and Archibald Constable are from here.

Important Allusion:

> "the Waverley Novels"--a term applied loosely to all of Scott's novels, of which *Waverley* (the hero's surname) was the first [1814]

Passing Allusion:

> Gustave Flaubert

- -

SECOND MARRIAGE (1918)   C105

Obvious Source:

> Viola Meynell, *Second Marriage*. Martin Secker, 1918.

- -

SIR THOMAS BROWNE (1923)   C235

Obvious Sources:

Works by Browne

(1) *Urn Burial*. (Orig. 1658)

(2) *The Garden of Cyrus*. (Orig. 1658)

(3) *Religio Medici*. (Orig. 1642)

All publ. by Waltham St. Lawrence, Berkshire: Golden Cockerel Pr., 1923.

Passing Allusions:

(1) Miscellaneous writers: Benjamin Disraeli, Samuel Pepys, Arthur Rimbaud

(2) G. Otto Trevelyan, *Life and Letters of Lord [Thomas Babington] Macaulay*. (Orig. 1876)

(3) Peter Beckford, *Thoughts on Hunting*. (Orig. 1781)

(4) James Henry Monk, *The Life of Richard Bentley, D.D.* (Orig. 1830)

(5) Arnold Bennett, *The Old Wives' Tale*. (Orig. 1908)

(6) John Galsworthy, *The Man of Property*. (Orig. 1906)

(7) "the nine volumes of M. [Marcel] Proust"

   A la Recherche du Temps Perdu. (Orig. 1914-[27])

- -

THE SISTER OF FREDERIC THE GREAT (1906)   C3.3

   Obvious Source: Reading notes
                                            B1a
   Edith E. Cuthell, *Wilhelmina Margravine of Bai-
   reuth*. 2 vol. Chapman and Hall, 1905.

   Specific quotes from:

   (1) "Thomas Carlyle finds"

      Carlyle, *History of Friedrich II of Prussia* ...
      7 vol. (Orig. 1869) Espec. Vols. V and VI.

   (2) "as Sainte-Beuve says"

      Charles Augustin Sainte-Beuve, "La Margrave
      de Bareith," in Sainte-Beuve, *Causeries du
      Lundi*. 15 vol. (Orig. 1851-62) Vol. XII.

   Passing Allusions:

      Miscellaneous European writers: Pierre Bayle,
      Gottfried Wilhelm Leibnitz, François Marie Arouet
      de Voltaire (mentioned by Cuthell)

- -

SMALL TALK ABOUT MEREDITH (1919)   C140

   Obvious Source:

      S[tewart] M[arsh] Ellis, *George Meredith. His Life
      and Friends in Relation to His Work*. Grant
      Richards, 1919.

Specific quote from:

"an interesting statement by [George Bernard Shaw]"

Shaw to Ellis, letter, n.d. given

Important Allusions (mentioned by Ellis):

Works by Meredith

(1) *Evan Harrington*. (Orig. 1861)

(2) *Modern Love*. (Orig. 1862)

(3) *The Egoist*. (Orig. 1879)

(4) *Beauchamp's Career*. (Orig. 1876 [1875])

Passing Allusions:

(1) Miscellaneous English novelists (mentioned by Ellis): George Eliot [pseud. of Mary Ann Evans], Thomas Love Peacock

(2) Miscellaneous novelists: Jane Austen, Leo Tolstoy

(3) Various Shakespeare characters: Hamlet, Falstaff

(4) Mentioned by Shaw (see above):

(a) Works by Meredith

(i) *Diana of the Crossways*. (Orig. 1885)

(ii) *The Shaving of Shagpat*. (Orig. 1855)

(b) Charles Dickens, *Our Mutual Friend*. (Orig. 1865)

- -

SMOKE RINGS AND ROUNDELAYS (1924)   C255.4

Obvious Source: Reading notes
                                   B2o
Smoke Rings and Roundelays, comp. by Wilfred Partington. Castle, 1924.

SOCIAL LIFE IN ENGLAND (1916)   C61

    Obvious Source:

        F[rederick] J[ohn] Foakes Jackson, *Social Life
        in England, 1750-1850.* Macmillan, 1916.

    Passing Allusions (mentioned by Jackson):

        Miscellaneous English writers: George Crabbe,
        Thomas Creevey, Charles Dickens, William Shake-
        speare, Robert Smith Surtees, Anthony Trollope

- -

SOME OF THE SMALLER MANOR HOUSES OF SUSSEX (1925) C269.3

    Obvious Source:

        Viscountess [Frances] Wolseley, *Some of the
        Smaller Manor Houses of Sussex.* London and Bos-
        ton: Medici Society, 1925.

- -

SOMEHOW GOOD (1908)   Se p. 180, KP

    Obvious Source:

        William De Morgan, *Somehow Good.* Heinemann,
        1908.

    Important Allusions:

        Other works by De Morgan:

        (1) *Joseph Vance.* (Orig. 1906)

        (2) *Alice-for-Short.* (Orig. 1907)

- -

THE SON OF ROYAL LANGBRITH (1904)   C01

    Obvious Source:

        W[illiam] D[ean] Howells, *The Son of Royal Lang-
        brith.* New York: Harpers, 1904.

STALKY'S REMINISCENCES (1928)   C298.1

    Obvious Source:

        L.C. Dunsterville, *Stalky's Reminiscences.*
        Cape, 1928.

    Important Allusions (mentioned by Dunsterville):

        (1) Rudyard Kipling, "Ave Imperatrix." (Orig.
            1882)

        (2) Stalky (character in Kipling, *Stalky and Co.*
            [*sic*; orig. 1899])

- -

STEEPLE-JACKS AND STEEPLEJACKING (1926)   C272.5

    Obvious Source:

        William Larkins, *Steeple-Jacks and Steeplejack-
        ing.* Cape, 1926.

- -

STENDHAL (1924)   C249

    Obvious Sources: Reading notes
                                        #19
        Works by Stendhal [pseud. of Marie Henri Beyle]:

        (1) *Journal*, ed. by Henri Debraye and Louis Roy-
            er. 1923. (Orig. 1888)   Vol. I, 1801-05.

        (2) *Le Rouge et le Noir*, ed. by Jules Marsan,
            w/preface by Paul Bourget. 2 vol. 1923.
            (Orig. 1831)

        (3) *Vie de Rossini.* [Followed by] *Notes d'un Di-
            lettante*, ed. by Henry Prunieres. 2 vol.
            1922. (Orig. 1824, 1867, respectively)

        All published by Paris: Champion.

    Passing Allusion (mentioned by Stendhal):

        William Shakespeare

STENDHAL (1925?; publ. in 1972)   C378

   Inferred Sources: Reading notes
                                          #18
       (1) "this splendid and monumental edition of
           Stendhal [pseud. of Marie Henri Beyle]"

           Oeuvres Complètes de Stendhal. Paris:
           Champion, 1913-[40].

           Specifically mentioned:

           Le Rouge et le Noir, ed. by Jules Marsan.
           2 vol. 1923. (Orig. 1831)

       (2) Stendhal, *The Life of Henri Brulard*, trans.
           by Catherine Alison Phillips. Jonathan Cape,
           [1925]. (Orig. 1890)

       Both are listed in the reading notes.

   Passing Allusions:

       (1) Miscellaneous French writers: Anatole France,
           Marcel Proust, Marie de Sévigné

       (2) "We print Madame de Lafayette [Marie Made-
           leine Motier] at one of our University
           Presses"

           E.g., *La Princesse de Clèves*, ed. by H. Ash-
           ton. Cambridge: University Pr., 1925. (Or-
           ig. 1678)

- -

STOPFORD BROOKE (1917)   C91.1

   Obvious Source:

       L[eonard] P[earsall] Jacks, *Life and Letters of
       Stopford Brooke*. 2 vol. Murray, 1917.

       Specific quotes from:

       (1) Brooke to Mrs. [Blanche] Montague Crackan-
           thorpe

           (a) July (?), 1896

               First quote is from here.

(b) Dec. 31, 1901

Paragraph 6, quote 1, is from here.

(2) "said Mr. Chesterton" (paragraph 4)

G[ilbert] K[eith] Chesterton, Review of S. Brooke, *The Poetry of Robert Browning* (Ibiter, 1902), in *The Daily News* (London), Sept. 25, 1902

(3) From Brooke's diary

(a) Apr. 10, 1908

Paragraph 5, quote 1, is from here.

(b) "he spoke with impatience" (paragraph 5)

Oct. 8, 1899

(c) June 20, 1901

Paragraph 6, quote 2, is from here.

(4) Rabindranath Tagore, *The Sadhana. The Realisation of Life.* (Orig. 1913)

Important Allusions:

(1) Mentioned by Brooke

"Lord Selborne's life"

[Roundell Palmer], Earl of Selborne, *Memorials*, ed. by [Lady Sophia M. Palmer]. 4 vol. Macmillan, 1896-98.

(2) Mentioned by Jacks

"the Seven Ages of Man"

William Shakespeare, *As You Like It*, II:vii: 139-66. (Orig. publ. 1623)

Passing Allusions (mentioned by Brooke):

Miscellaneous writers: Henrik Ibsen, William Morris, John Ruskin

THE STRANGER IN LONDON (1908)   C15

    Obvious Sources:

        (1) A. Rutari [pseud. of Arthur Levy], *Londoner Skizzenbuch*. Leipzig: Degener, 1906.

        (2) Ch[arles] Huard, *Londres Comme Je l'Ai Vu*. Paris: Rey, 1908.

    Important Allusion (mentioned by Rutari and Huard):

        Charles Dickens

    Passing Allusions:

        (1) Miscellaneous writers

            (a) Mentioned by Rutari and Huard: Joseph Addison, Charles Lamb, William Shakespeare

            (b) Mentioned by Rutari: Henrik Ibsen, Dr. Samuel Johnson, Friederich Nietzsche, Leo Tolstoy

        (2) Mentioned by Rutari

        The Spectator (periodical, 1711-12)

- -

THE SUNSET [*re* Leslie Stephen] (1906)   B1

    Important Allusions:

        (1) Works by Sir Walter Scott

            (a) *Guy Mannering*. (Orig. 1815)

            (b) *The Heart of Midlothian*. (Orig. 1818)

        (2) William Makepeace Thackeray, *Vanity Fair*. (Orig. 1848)

        (3) John Milton, "On the Morning of Christ's Nativity." (Orig. 1645)

        (4) George Meredith, "Love in the Valley." (Orig. 1851)

        (5) Sir Alfred Lyall, *Verses Written in India*. (Orig. 1889)

(6) Henry Newbolt, "Admirals All." (Orig. 1897)

(7) Matthew Arnold, "The Scholar Gipsy." (Orig. 1853)

(8) Plato

Passing Allusions:

(1) Thomas Hughes, *Tom Brown's School Days*. (Orig. 1857)

(2) Robert Louis Stevenson, *Treasure Island*. (Orig. 1883)

(3) Thomas Carlyle, *The French Revolution*. (Orig. 1837)

(4) Miscellaneous writers: Jane Austen, Johann Wolfgang von Goethe, Nathaniel Hawthorne, Heinrich Heine, John Keats, Rudyard Kipling, William Shakespeare, Alfred Lord Tennyson, William Wordsworth

- -

SUNSET REFLECTIONS (1917)   C95

Obvious Source:

E.M. Martin, *The Happy Fields*. Stratford-upon-Avon: Shakespeare Head, 1917.

Passing Allusion (mentioned by Martin):

William Shakespeare

- -

A SUPREME MOMENT (1906)   C3.5

Obvious Source: Reading notes
                                   B1a
Mrs. Hamilton Synge, *A Supreme Moment*. Fisher Unwin, 1905.

A SWAN AND HER FRIENDS (1907)   C7

    Obvious Source:

        E[dward] V[errall] Lucas, *A Swan and Her Friends*.
        Methuen, 1907.

        Specific quotes from:

        (1) Anna Seward's letters

            (a) *Re* sister Sarah

                To unstated correspondent, 1764

                There should be ellipses between "pen-
                sive" and "laughed"; instead of ellipses
                after "once," there should be a dash.

            (b) *Re* mother, Elizabeth Hunter Seward

                Ibid.

                There should be ellipses between "I" and
                "grew," and "she" and "took"; no ellipses
                between "mother" and "that."

            (c) "Miss Seward dub[s] herself"

                To Thomas Sedgwick Whalley, n.d.

                Cannot locate

        (2) William Hayley, "'the Bard of Sussex,' ...
        laugh[s] ... over [Seward]"

            Hayley to Eliza Hayley, Dec. 18, 1781; repr.
            in Hayley, *Memoirs of the Life and Writings
            of ...*, ed. by John Johnson. 2 vol. Simp-
            kin and Marshall, 1823. Vol. I.

        (3) Comments by Sir Walter Scott

            (a) Scott to Joanna Baillie, March 18, 1810;
                repr. in J[ohn] G[ibson] Lockhart, *Mem-
                oirs of the Life of Scott*. Vol. III;
                "with" before "despair" should not be in
                quote marks

                (See "Scott's Character,")

            (b) Scott, "Prefatory Memoir" to Seward, *Po-
                etical Works*. 3 vol. Edinburgh: James
                Ballantyne, 1810.

                Final quote is from here; "with a" should
                be in brackets.

Supportive Source:

> Thomas Babington Macaulay, *Marginal Notes*, ed.
> by G[eorge] O[tto] Trevelyan. Longmans, 1907.
>
> This is listed in Holleyman.
>
> Specific quote from:
>
> *Re* Seward's letter on Latin writers
>
> Anna Seward to Sophia Weston, Feb. 9, 1790; re-
> pr. in Seward, *Letters ... 1784-1807*. 6 vol.
> Edinburgh: Archibald Constable, 1811. Vol. II.

Important Allusions (mentioned by Seward):

> Miscellaneous writers: Horace, Mrs. Piozzi [Hes-
> ter Lynch Thrale], Virgil

Passing Allusions:

> (1) Miss Bates (character in Jane Austen, *Emma*
>   [1816])
>
> (2) Mentioned by Lucas:
>
>> (a) "what Lamb said about Miss Benjay [*sic*;
>>   i.e., Elizabeth Ogilvy Benger]"
>>
>>   Charles Lamb to Samuel Taylor Coleridge,
>>   Apr. 16/17, 1800
>>
>> (b) Miss Barbara Pinkerton (character in
>>   William Makepeace Thackeray, *Vanity Fair*
>>   [1848])
>
> (3) Mentioned by Seward (mentioned also by Lu-
>   cas):
>
>   Miscellaneous minor English writers: Christo-
>   pher Anstey, Robert Potter [translator of
>   Aeschylus]
>
> (4) Mentioned by Scott: Samuel Johnson

- -

SWEETNESS--LONG DRAWN OUT (1906)   C5.6

> Obvious Source: Reading notes
>   B1a
>   Marie Hay, *A German Pompadour*. Constable, 1906.

SWINBURNE LETTERS (1918)   C103

    Obvious Source:

        Thomas Hake and Arthur Compton Rickett, eds.,
        The Letters of Algernon Charles Swinburne. With
        Some Personal Recollections. Murray, 1918.

        Specific quotes from:

        (1) Paragraph 2

            Swinburne to Dante Gabriel Rossetti:

            (a) "Here it is a question"; "too soon and
                suddenly" should be in quote marks

                Dec. 10, 1869

                Quotes 3 and 5 are also from here; "in
                the Haymarket" should read "on the Hay-
                market."

            (b) "Here it is a matter"

                Feb. 24, 1870

                Quote 4 is also from here.

        (2) Paragraph 3

            (a) *Re* Society for the Suppression of Vice

                Swinburne to Benjamin Jowett, July 7,
                1875

            (b) *Re* Captain Matthew Webb

                Swinburne to Theodore Watts-Dunton, Aug.
                27, 1875

    Important Allusion (mentioned by editors):

        Swinburne, *Love's Cross Currents.* (Orig. 1901)

    Passing Allusions:

        (1) Miscellaneous writers:

            (a) Lord Byron, John Keats

            (b) Mentioned by Swinburne: Homer, François
                Rabelais, William Shakespeare, Percy
                Bysshe Shelley

(2) Works by William Cowper:

    (a) *The Task*. (Orig. 1785)

    (b) *The Correspondence of* ... , arr. by
        Thomas Wright. (Orig. 1904)

(3) Mentioned by Swinburne:

    William Morris, *The Earthly Paradise*. (Orig. 1868-70)

- -

THE TALE OF GENJI (1925)   C264

  Obvious Source:

    Lady Shikibu Murasaki, *The Tale of Genji*, trans.
    by Arthur Waley. Vol. I. Allen and Unwin, 1925.

Important Allusions:

(1) Works by Aelfric:

    (a) *The Catholic Homilies*. (Orig. c.990-94)

    (b) *Treatise on the Old and New Testaments*.
        (Orig. 1005-12)

(2) "Sumer Is Icumen In"

    Anonymous lyric. (Orig. c.1250)

Passing Allusions:

    Miscellaneous European novelists: Miguel de Cer-
    vantes Saavedra, Leo Tolstoi

- -

A TALKER (1917)   C72

  Obvious Source:

    Edgar Lee Masters, *The Great Valley*. T. Werner
    Laurie, 1916.

(1) Specific poems quoted from:

    (a) "Autochthon" (first 2 quotes)

    (b) "Cato Braden"

    (c) "Marsyas"

    (d) "Apollo at Pherae"

    (e) "Steam Shovel Cut"

    (f) "Come, Republic"

(2) Poems mentioned but not quoted from:

    (a) "[also] about Cato Braden"

       "Will Boyden Lectures"

    (b) "Malachy Degan"

    (c) "Slip Shoe Lovey"

Passing Allusions:

(1) Jerry Ott (character in "Cato Braden" [see above])

(2) Robert Browning

- -

TCHEHOV'S QUESTIONS (1918)   C107

Obvious Sources:

Works by Anton Tchehov:

(1) *The Wife and Other Stories*, trans. by Constance Garnett. Chatto and Windus, 1918.

(2) *The Witch and Other Stories*, trans. by Constance Garnett. Chatto and Windus, 1918.

(3) *Nine Humorous Tales*, trans. by Isaac Goldberg and Henry T. Schnittkind. Boston: Stratford, 1918.

Specific stories quoted from:

(1) "The Post." (Orig. 1887) In *The Witch and Other Stories*.

(2) Paragraph 4

(a) "Agafya." (Orig. 1886) In *ibid.*

(b) "The Wife." (Orig. 1892)

Specific stories mentioned but not quoted from:

(1) "A Dreary Story." (Orig. 1889) In *The Wife and Other Stories.*

(2) "Gusev." (Orig. 1890) In *The Witch and Other Stories.*

Passing Allusions:

Miscellaneous writers

(1) Mentioned by translator(s) of *Nine Humorous Tales*: O. Henry [pseud. of William Sidney Porter], Guy de Maupassant

(2) Fyodor Dostoevsky

- -

TEMPTATION (1907)   C5.9

Obvious Source:

Richard Bagot, *Temptation.* Methuen, 1906.

- -

THEIR PASSING HOUR (1905)   C2.3

Obvious Source: Reading notes
                                   B1a
John Fyvie, *Some Famous Women of Wit and Beauty.* Constable, 1905.

Specific quotes from:

(1) *Re* Caroline Sheridan Norton

Fanny Kemble, *Records of a Girlhood.* 3 vol. (Orig. 1878-79). Vol. III.

(2) *Ibid.*

"She had" should be in brackets.

(3) *Ibid.*

"She was" should read "Mrs. Norton was."

(4) *Journal of Rear-Admiral Bartholomew James.*
(Orig. 1896)

(5) Mrs. St. George [pseud. of Melesina Trench],
Journal Kept During a Visit to Germany ... ,
ed. by Dean R.C. Trench. (Orig. 1861)

(6) "[Samuel] Johnson said [Elizabeth Montagu]"

Fanny Burney, *Diary and Letters....* 7 vol.
(Orig. 1842, 1846) Vol. I.

[Late August or early September], 1778

(7) Lady Elizabeth Eastlake's "criticism of
John Ruskin"

Unsigned review of Ruskin, *Modern Painters*,
Vols. I-III, in *Quarterly Review*, 98 (March
1856), 384-432

(8) "Mr. Meredith ... desires"

George Meredith, *Diana of the Crossways.*
(Orig. 1885) Prefatory note to Edition de
Luxe. Archibald Constable, 1897.

Supportive Source:

"says George Meredith" (paragraph 1)

Cannot locate

Important Allusions (mentioned by Fyvie):

(1) Elizabeth Montagu, *An Essay on the Writings
and Genius of Shakespear.* (Orig. 1769)

(2) Charlotte Lennox, *The Female Quixote....*
(Orig. 1752)

(3) Lady Marguerite Blessington

THESE WERE MUSES (1924)   C256.3

    Obvious Source:

        Mona Wilson, *These Were Muses*. Sidgwick and
        Jackson, 1924.

    Important Allusions (mentioned by Wilson):

        Miscellaneous British writers: Susannah Cent-
        livre, Sara Coleridge, Lady Sydney Morgan, Fran-
        ces Sheridan, Frances Trollope

- -

THIS FOR REMEMBRANCE (1925)   C260.01

    Obvious Source:

        Bernard [John Seymour], Lord Coleridge, *This for
        Remembrance*. T. Fisher Unwin, 1925.

- -

THREE CHARACTERS (1930; publ. 1972)   C377

    Passing Allusions:

        Miscellaneous writers: Aristotle, Marie Corelli,
        John Keats, Plato, Sir Walter Scott, William
        Shakespeare

- -

TIME, TASTE, AND FURNITURE (1925)   C265.4

    Obvious Source:

        John Gloag, *Time, Taste, and Furniture*. Grant
        Richards, 1925.

TOLSTOY'S "THE COSSACKS" (1917)   C64

Obvious Source:

Leo Tolstoy, *The Cossacks and Other Tales of the Caucasus,* trans. by Louise and Aylmer Maude. World Classics ser. Oxford: University Pr.; London: Milford, 1916.

Specific stories quoted from:

(1) "The Cossacks." (Orig. 1863)

First 3 quotes are from here.

(2) Quote 4

"The Raid." (Orig. 1852)

Passing Allusions:

(1) Miscellaneous fictionists: Charles Dickens, Fyodor Dostoevsky, Guy de Maupassant, Prosper Mérimée, Anton Tchekov, William Makepeace Thackeray

(2) Various Tolstoy characters: Daddy Eroshka, Lukashka, Dimitri Olenin (in *The Cossacks*); Pierre Bezrakhov (in *War and Peace* [1868]); Konstantin Levin (in *Anna Karenina* [1873-77])

- -

TO READ OR NOT TO READ (1917)   C85

Obvious Source:

Viscount [Ernest] Harberton, *How to Lengthen Our Ears.* C.W. Daniel, 1917.

Important Allusions (mentioned by Harberton):

Miscellaneous scientific writers: Charles Darwin, Thomas Huxley

Passing Allusions (mentioned by Harberton):

Miscellaneous writers: Edward Gibbon, Oliver Goldsmith, Arthur Schopenhauer, Algernon Charles Swinburne, William Wordsworth

THE TOWER OF SILOAM (1905)   C2.15

    Obvious Source: Reading notes
                                       B1a
        Mrs. [Alice] Henry Graham, *The Tower of Siloam.*
        Alston Rivers, 1905.

    Passing Allusions:

        Miscellaneous English novelists: E[dward] F[red-
        eric] Benson, Anthony Hope

- -

TRAFFICKS AND DISCOVERIES (1906)   C5.7

    Obvious Source: Reading notes
                                       B1a
        Walter Raleigh, *English Voyages of the Sixteenth*
        Century. Glasgow: James MacLehose, 1906.

    Supportive Source:

        "those five cumbrous volumes [of Hakluyt]"

        [Richard Hakluyt, ed.] *Hakluyt's Collection of*
        the Early Voyages, Travels, and Discoveries of
        the English Nation. New ed. 5 vol. R.H. Evans,
        1809-12. (Orig. 1598-1600)

        This is listed in Holleyman Addendum II; it be-
        longed to Virginia.

    Passing Allusions (mentioned by Raleigh):

        Miscellaneous 16th-century playwrights: Christo-
        pher Marlowe, William Shakespeare

- -

TRAFFICKS AND DISCOVERIES (1918)   C133

    Obvious Sources: Reading notes
                                       B2d
        (1) J[ames] A[nthony] Froude, *English Seamen in*
            the Sixteenth Century. Longmans, 1918.
            (Orig. 1895)

(2) *The [sic] Hakluyt's Voyages, Travels, and Discoveries of the English Nation*, ed. by Richard Hakluyt. (Orig. 1598-1600)

Poss. ed.: See "Trafficks and Discoveries [1906]," above.

Passing Allusion:

Homer, *The Odyssey*. (Orig. 10th cent. B.C.)

- -

THE TRAGIC LIFE OF VINCENT VAN GOGH (1925)   C262.3

Obvious Source:

Louis Piérard, *The Tragic Life of Vincent Van Gogh*, trans. by Herbert Garland. Castle, 1925.

Important Allusion (mentioned by Garland):

"the standard life by Meier-Graefe"

Julius Meier-Graefe, *Vincent van Gogh*, trans. by John Holroyd Reece. 2 vol. London, Boston: Medici Society, 1922.

- -

TROUSERS (1921)   C222

Obvious Source:

A. Trystan Edwards, *The Things Which Are Seen*. Philip Allan, 1921.

Passing Allusion:

The New Statesman (periodical, 1913-[31])

- -

THE TRUTH AT LAST (1924)   C250.1

Obvious Source:

Charles Hawtrey, *The Truth at Last*, w/intro. by Somerset Maugham. Thornton Butterworth, 1924.

TWENTY YEARS OF MY LIFE (1925)   C268.2

    Obvious Source:

        Louise Jopling-Rowe, *Twenty Years of My Life*.
        Bodley Head, 1925.

    Passing Allusion (mentioned by Jopling-Rowe):

        Oscar Wilde

- -

TWO IRISH NOVELS (1905)   C2.14

    Obvious Sources: Reading notes
                                          B1a
        (1) Shan F. Bullock, *Dan the Dollar*.   Dublin:
        Maunsel, 1905.

        (2) Louise Kenny, *The Red Haired Woman*.   Murray,
        1905.

- -

TWO IRISH POETS (1918)   C106

    Obvious Sources:

        (1) Francis Ledwidge, *Last Songs*.   Herbert Jen-
        kins, 1918.

        Specific poems quoted from (paragraph 2):

        (a) "The Find."

        (b) "To One Who Comes Now and Then."

        (c) "With Flowers."

        (2) James Stephens, *Reincarnations*.   Macmillan,
        1918.

        Specific quotes from (paragraph 3):

        (a) "Note" [in back].

        (b) *Ibid*.

   (c) "Peggy Mitchell." ["After (Antoine)
       Raftery." Orig. in Gaelic, 18th cent.]

   (d) "Righteous Anger." ["After (David)
       O'Bruadair." Orig. in Gaelic, 17th
       cent.]

Important Allusion:

   Lord Dunsany [Edward John Morton Drax Plunkett]

Passing Allusions:

   Miscellaneous Irish writers: Egan O'Rahilly
   (mentioned by Stephens), John Millington Synge

- -

THE TWO SAMUEL BUTLERS (1925)   C260.1

   Obvious Source:

       Samuel Butler, *The Life and Letters of Dr. Samuel
       Butler*. 2 vol. Shrewsbury ed. Cape, 1925.

   Important Allusions:

   Works by Samuel Butler (19th cent.)

   (1) *The Way of All Flesh*. (Orig. 1903)

   (2) *The Note-Books*. (Orig. 1912)

   Passing Allusions (mentioned by Butler):

   Miscellaneous writers: Aeschylus, Charles Darwin

- -

UNKNOWN ESSEX (1925)   C265.2

   Obvious Source:

       Donald Maxwell, *Unknown Essex*. Bodley Head,
       1925.

UNPUBLISHED LETTERS OF MATTHEW ARNOLD (1924)   C244.2

Obvious Source:

Matthew Arnold, *Unpublished Letters of ...* , ed.
by Arnold Whitridge.   New Haven, Conn.: Yale U.
Pr.; London: Milford, 1923.

Specific quotes from:

(1) Arnold to Jane Arnold Forster, n.d. [1849?]

(2) Same to same, May 22, 1859

Important Allusion (mentioned by Whitridge):

Arnold, "The Strayed Reveller." (Orig. 1849)

Passing Allusions (mentioned by Arnold):

Miscellaneous writers: Aristotle, William Wordsworth

- -

UNWRITTEN HISTORY (1924)   C246.4

Obvious Source:

Cosmo Hamilton, *Unwritten History*.   Hutchinson,
1924.

- -

VALERY BRUSSOF (1918)   C128

Obvious Source:

Valery Brussof, *The Republic of the Southern
Cross and Other Stories*, w/intro. by Stephen
Graham.   Constable, 1918.

Specific quotes from:

(1) Quoted by Graham:

"[Brussof] has expressed his belief that";
there should be ellipses between "boundary"
and "between"

Brussof, Preface to *The Axis of the Earth*.
2nd ed. Moscow: Scorpion[?], 1910. (Orig.
1907)

(2) Specific stories quoted from:

(a) "he makes his Roman lovers ask"

"Rhea Silvia." (Orig. 1914)

(b) "the old tramp ... answers"

"The Marble Bust." (Orig. 1903)

- -

A VANISHED GENERATION (1908)   C21

Obvious Source:

Memoirs of a Vanished Generation, 1813-1855,
ed. by Mrs. Warrenne Blake, w/intro. by Lady
Mary St. Helier. Lane, 1908.

Supportive Source:

"Captain Mahan's biography [of Lord Horatio Nel-
son]"

A[lfred] T[hayer] Mahan, *The Life of Nelson*....
Prob. ed.: 2nd ed. rev. Sampson Low, 1899.
(Orig. 1897)

This is listed in Holleyman; it belonged to Leslie Stephen.

- -

VENICE (1909)   C28

Obvious Source:

Pompeo Molmenti, *Venice*, Parts II and III ["*The
Golden Ages*" and "*The Decadence*"], trans. by
Horatio Brown. 4 vol. Murray, 1907-08. (Orig.
1880)

Supportive Source:

"as Ruskin called it"

John Ruskin, *The Stones of Venice.* (Orig. 1851,
1853) Prob. ed.: Travellers' Ed. 2 vol.
George Allen, 1904.

This is listed in Holleyman.

Important Allusion:

"The first part of Signor Molmenti's work"

I.e.,"*The Middle Ages.*" 2 vol. (Orig. 1880)

Passing Allusion (mentioned by Molmenti):

Carlo Goldoni

- -

A VICTORIAN ECHO (1917)   C83

Obvious Source:

Thomas Gordon Hake, *Parables and Tales.* Elkin
Mathews, 1917. (Orig. 1873)

(1) Specific poems quoted from:

(a) Paragraph 2

"The Lily of the Valley."

(b) Paragraph 5

(i) *Ibid.*

There should be ellipses after
"out."

(ii) *Ibid.*

(iii) "The Blind Boy."

(2) Specific poem mentioned but not quoted from:

"Old Souls."

Supportive Source:

"the claim that Rossetti made for [Hake]"

Dante Gabriel Rossetti, "Dr. Hake's Poems,"
Fortnightly Review, 19 (Apr. 1873), 537ff.; repr. in Rossetti, *The Collected Works of ...* ,
ed. by William M. Rossetti. (Orig. 1886) Prob.
ed.: Ellis and Elvey, 1901.

This is listed in Holleyman; it belonged to Virginia.

Passing Allusions:

Miscellaneous English writers

(1) Mentioned by D.G. Rossetti: John Bunyan,
Thomas Gray, Alexander Pope, Francis Quarles,
William Wordsworth

(2) Alice Meynell

- -

VICTORIAN JOTTINGS (1927)   C279.1

Obvious Source:

Sir James Crichton-Browne, *Victorian Jottings*.
Etchells and Macdonald, 1926.

Passing Allusion (mentioned by Crichton-Browne):

Thomas Huxley

- -

A VICTORIAN SOCIALIST (1918)   C113

Obvious Source:

Ernest Belfort Bax, *Reminiscences and Reflections
of a Mid and Late Victorian*. George Allen and
Unwin, 1918.

Important Allusion (mentioned by Bax):

William Morris

A VIEW OF THE RUSSIAN REVOLUTION (1918)   C135

    Obvious Source:

        Meriel Buchanan, *Petrograd: The City of Trouble,
        1914-1918*, [w/foreword by Hugh Walpole]. Col-
        lins, 1918.

- -

THE WAR FROM THE STREET (1919)   C139

    Obvious Source:

        D. Bridgman Metchim, *Our Own History of the War.
        From a South London View*. Stockwell, 1918.

        Specific quote from:

        "[George Bernard] Shaw said"

        Cannot locate

- -

WASHINGTON IRVING (1919)   C146

    Obvious Source:

        Washington Irving, *Tales of* ... , sel. and ed.
        by Carl Van Doren. Milford, 1918.

        Specific story mentioned:

        "The Stout Gentleman." (Orig. 1822)

    Passing Allusions:

        (1) Miscellaneous writers: William Shakespeare,
            Walt Whitman

        (2) *Ruth* (in Old Testament)

WATTS-DUNTON'S DILEMMA (1919)   C177

  Obvious Source:

    Coulson Kernahan, *Swinburne As I Knew Him*. John
    Lane, 1919.

    Specific quote from (mentioned by Watts-Dunton):

    "Shakespeare's brown October [i.e., ale or beer]"

    Cannot locate; Shakespeare applies "brown" to
    Spanish wine, according to concordance(s)

  Important Allusions:

    Miscellaneous English writers: Algernon Charles
    Swinburne, Theodore Watts-Dunton

  Passing Allusions (mentioned by Kernahan):

    (1) Miscellaneous writers: Victor Hugo, Alfred
        Lord Tennyson

    (2) Mrs. Grundy (character in Thomas Morton,
        Speed the Plough [1800])

- -

THE WEEK END (1924)   C248

  Obvious Source:

    The Week End Book, [ed. by Vera Mendel and Sir
    Francis Meynell]. Nonesuch Pr., 1924.

    Specific quotes from:

    (1) "an embarrassing statement"

        John Donne, "Love's Growth." (Orig. 1633)

    (2) "a 'great poem'"

        Ralph Waldo Emerson, "Days." (Orig. 1857)

  Passing Allusions (mentioned in book, *passim*);

    (1) Miscellaneous English poets: John Keats,
        William Shakespeare, Percy Bysshe Shelley

    (2) "a living rhymer ... [who] wrote 'great poems'"

        Identity uncertain

A WEEK IN THE WHITE HOUSE (1908)   C25

    Obvious Source:

        William Bayard Hale, *A Week in the White House
        with Theodore Roosevelt.* New York and London:
        G.P. Putnam's, 1908.

    Passing Allusions (mentioned by Hale):

        (1) J[ohn] J[ames] Ingalls, "Opportunity."
            (Orig. 1891)

        (2) Jonathan Edwards

- -

WHAT IS A NOVEL? (1927)   C280.2

    Important Allusion:

        H[erbert] G[eorge] Wells, *The World of William
        Clissold.* 3 vol. Ernest Benn, 1926.

    Passing Allusions:

        Miscellaneous writers: Walter de la Mare, Elinor
        Glyn, Thomas Hardy, Rudyard Kipling, Marcel
        Proust

- -

WILLIAM ALLINGHAM (1907)   C8

    Obvious Source:

        William Allingham: A Diary, ed. by H. Allingham
        and D. Radford. Macmillan, 1907.

    Specific quotes from:

    (1) "Allingham's autobiography"

        I.e., first one-and-a-half chapters of book

        First 4 quotes are from here.

    (2) "Leigh Hunt ... exclaimed"

Entry of June 27, 1847

There should be ellipses between "fellow"
and "Carlyle," and before "I will"

(3) *Re* Alfred Lord Tennyson

(a) Entry of June 28, 1851

There should be ellipses between "broad-
shouldered"and "man"; "the best" should
read "best"

(b) *Re* fig tree

Entry of Oct. 3, 1863

(c) *Re* Tennyson, *Maud*. (Orig. 1855)

Entry of June 25, 1865

(4) *Re* Thomas Carlyle

(a) "Carlyle is heard"

Entry of Oct. 16, 1867

(b) Carlyle on Percy Bysshe Shelley

Entry of Dec. 27, 1875

(c) Carlyle on Algernon Charles Swinburne

Entry of Oct. 27, 1877

(d) Carlyle on J.M. Whistler

Entry of July 29, 1873

(e) Carlyle on Walt Whitman

Entry of Oct. 3, 1872

(f) Carlyle on William Shakespeare

(i) Entry of Nov. 8, 1871

(ii) *Re Othello*. (Orig. publ. 1622)

Entry of Apr. 19, 1880

(g) Carlyle on own works (see below)

Entry of Jan. 23, 1874

(5) "as George Eliot said"

   Entry of Apr. 19, 1880

Important Allusions (mentioned by Carlyle):

   Works by self

   (1) *Sartor Resartus*. (Orig. 1836)

   (2) *Oliver Cromwell's Letters and Speeches*.
       (Orig. 1845)

Passing Allusions:

   (1) Mentioned by Hunt: Robert Browning, Charles
       Dickens

   (2) Mentioned by Tennyson: George Meredith, *Love
       in the Valley*. (Orig. 1851)

- -

WORDSWORTH AND THE LAKES (1906)   C5

   Obvious Sources: Reading notes
                                      B1a
   (1) *Wordsworth's Guide to the Lakes*, w/intro.
       and ed. by Ernest de Selincourt. 5th ed.
       Frowde, 1906. (Orig. 1810; 1835 in 5th ed.)

   (2) H.D. Rawnsley, *Months at the Lakes*. Glasgow:
       MacLehose, 1906.

- -

WORDSWORTH LETTERS (1908)   C13

   Obvious Source:

       *Letters of the Wordsworth Family. From 1787 to
       1855*, coll. and ed. by William Knight. 3 vol.
       Boston and London: Ginn, 1907.

   Specific letters quoted from:

   (1) Paragraph 2

(a) "printed here for the first time"

William Wordsworth to Samuel Taylor Coleridge, [Dec. 24, 1799]

(b) Quote 2:

Ibid.

(c) Quote 3:

Re Wordsworth and Coleridge, *Lyrical
Ballads.* (Orig. 1798)

Ibid.

(d) Quote 4:

Same to same, Apr. 19, 1808

(e) Quote 5:

Re Horace Walpole

Same to Alexander Dyce, March 20, 1833

(f) Quote 6:

Re Thomas Carlyle and Ralph Waldo Emerson

Same to Henry Reed, Aug. 16, 1841

(g) Quote 7:

Same to William Rowan Hamilton, Jan. 4,
1838

(2) Paragraph 3

(a) Quote 2:

Dorothy Wordsworth to Jane Pollard, Feb.
16, 1793

(b) Quote 3:

Same to Mrs. [Catherine] Clarkson, Aug.
15, 1816

(c) Quote 4:

William Wordsworth to Thomas De Quincey,
March 6, 1804

(d) Quote 5:

Re Coleridge

Same to Thomas Poole, [c. May 1809(?)];
"it you" should read "it to you";
"proofs that" should read "proofs which"

(e) Quote 6:

Same to Lady [Constance] Beaumont, May
21, 1807; "for poetry" should read "of
poetry"

(3) Paragraph 4

(a) Quotes 1 and 4:

Cannot locate

(b) Quote 2:

William Wordsworth to Sir George Beaumont, Apr. 8, [1808]; there should be
ellipses after "white"

(c) Quote 3:

Same to Mary Hutchinson Wordsworth, July
5, [1837]

Passing Allusions:

Miscellaneous British letter-writers: Jane Welsh
Carlyle, Edward FitzGerald, Charles Lamb

- -

THE WRONG WAY OF READING (1920)*   C194

Obvious Source:

Constance Hill, *Mary Russell Mitford and Her
Surroundings*. Lane, 1920.

Specific quotes from:

(1) Paragraph 1

Re Alresford

Cannot locate quotes within quote

(b) "Miss Mitford writes"; "house" should read "home" (mistake by Hill)

Mitford, *Recollections of a Literary Life*. 3 vol. Richard Bentley, 1852. Vol. I.

(2) Paragraph 4

(a) "[Miss Mitford] wrote [*re* pony chaise]"

To Emily Jephson, July 10, 1824; repr. in *The Life of Mary Russell Mitford, Told by Herself in Letters to Her Friends*, ed. by A.G.K. L'Estrange. 3 vol. Richard Bentley, 1870. Vol. II.

(b) "she exclaimed"

Miss Mitford to Dr. George Mitford, July 5, 1811; repr. in *ibid*. Vol. I.

Should read: "I would not exchange my father ... for any man on earth, though he could pour all the gold of Peru into my lap."

Supportive Sources:

(1) "[Mrs. Mary Mitford(?)] sighed" (paragraph 4)

Cannot locate

(2) *Re* glow-worms

Miss Mitford to James Payn, n.d. given; repr. in Payn, *Some Literary Recollections*. Smith, Elder, 1884.

This is listed in Holleyman Addendum; it belonged to Leslie Stephen.

There should be ellipses before and after "that." ("K." is her maid, a Mrs. Kerenhappuch Swetman.)

(3) "a letter to a literary young man [i.e., Payn]"

In *ibid*.; n.d. given. "Keats, Wordsworth and myself" should read "I and Wordsworth and Keats." Sentence "Do ... love!" is a manufactured quote based on opinions of Miss Mitford paraphrased by Payn.

(4) Charles Kingsley to James Payn; in *ibid.*, n.d. given [post-1854]

All quotes, paragraph 5, are from here.

Important Allusion (mentioned by Mitford):

Mary Russell Mitford, *Our Village*. (Orig. 1824)

Passing Allusions:

(1) Alexander Pope

(2) Miscellaneous writers (mentioned by Mitford): Inez de Castro, John Keats, Petrarch [Domenico Petrarca]

(3) William Wordsworth and Samuel Taylor Coleridge, *Lyrical Ballads*. (Orig. 1798)

* This essay contributed to "Miss Mitford" in *Common Reader I*.

- -

APPENDICES

LOCATION KEY TO ESSAYS INDEXED

1. "Abraham Lincoln," *TLS* , Oct. 31, 1918, p. 523.

2. "Adventurers All," *TLS* , Oct. 10, 1918, p. 477.

3. "After His Kind," *Guardian*, Jan. 10, 1906, p. 89.

4. "An American Poet," *TLS*, Jan. 29, 1920, p. 64.

5. "The American Woman," *Guardian*, May 31, 1905, p. 939.

6. "Among the Poets," *TLS*, Nov. 2, 1916, p. 523.

7. "Anatole France," *Nation and Athenaeum*, May 3, 1924, p. 154.

8. "Anon," *Twentieth Century Literature*, 25 (Fall/Winter 1979), 380-424.

9. "Appreciations," *Nation and Athenaeum*, Sept. 27, 1924, pp. 782-83.

10. "Arrows of Fortune," *Guardian*, May 10, 1905, p. 803.

11. "Art and Life," *TLS*, Aug. 5, 1909, p. 284.

12. "Arthur Yates," *Nation and Athenaeum*, Feb 16, 1924. p. 724.

13. "The Author's Progress," *Guardian*, July 25, 1906, p. 1254.

14. "Bad Writers," *TLS*, Nov. 21, 1918, p. 566.

15. "'Barham of Beltana,'" *TLS*, March 17, 1905, p. 90.

16. "Before the Mast--and After," *Nation and Athenaeum*, July 12, 1924, p. 490.

17. "Behind the Brass Plate," *Nation and Athenaeum*, May 5, 1928, p. 152.

18. "Behind the Scenes with Cyril Maude," *Nation and Athenaeum*, Apr. 28, 1928, p. 120.

19. "A Belle of the Fifties," *Guardian*, Feb. 8, 1905, p. 247.

20. "'Blackstick Papers,'" *TLS*, Nov. 19, 1908, p. 411.

21. "Blanche Esmead," *TLS*, March 23, 1906, p. 104.

22. "The Bluest of the Blue," *Guardian*, July 11, 1906, p. 1179.

23. "The Book of Catherine Wells," *Nation and Athenaeum*, May 26, 1928, p. 260.

24. "A Book of Essays," *TLS*, Jan. 17, 1918, p. 31.

25. "The Brown House and Cordelia," *Guardian*, Dec. 6, 1905, pp. 2085-86.

26. "By Beach and Bogland," *Guardian*, March 22, 1905, pp. 507-08.

27. "Byron and Mr. Briggs," *Yale Review*, n.s. 68 (March 1979), 325-49.

28. "A Cambridge V.A.D.," *TLS*, May 10, 1917, p. 223.

29. "The Candle of Vision," *TLS*, Oct. 31, 1918, p. 522.

30. "Celebrities of Our Times," *Nation and Athenaeum*, May 16, 1925, p. 214.

31. "The 'Censorship' of Books," *Nineteenth Century and After*, April 1929, pp. 446-47.

32. "A Character Sketch," *Athenaeum*, Aug. 13, 1920, pp. 201-02.

33. "Charlotte Brontë," *TLS*, Apr. 13, 1916, pp. 169-70.

34. "Charlotte Brontë," *TLS*, Dec. 13, 1917, p. 615.

35. "Chateau and Country Life," *TLS*, Oct. 29, 1908, p. 375.

36. "The Cherry Orchard," *New Statesman*, July 24, 1920, pp. 446-47.

37. "The Chinese Shoe," *Nation and Athenaeum*, Nov. 17, 1923, pp. 277-78.

38. "Chinese Stories," *TLS*, May 1, 1913, p. 184.

39. "Clara Butt: Her Life Story," *Nation and Athenaeum*, July 14, 1928, p. 506.

40. "The Compromise," *TLS*, June 15, 1906, p. 217.

41. "Congreve," *New Statesman*, Apr. 2, 1921, p. 756.

42. "Congreve," *Nation and Athenaeum*, Oct. 17, 1925, p. 124.

43. "Coniston," *TLS*, July 13, 1906, p. 249.

44. "A Cookery Book," *TLS*, Nov. 25, 1909, p. 457.

45. "*Les Copains*," *TLS*, Aug. 7, 1913, p. 330.

46. "The Cornish Miner," *Nation and Athenaeum*, Feb. 25, 1928, p. 792.

47. "Creative Criticism," *TLS*, June 7, 1917, p. 271.

48. "A Dark Lantern," *Guardian*, May 24, 1905, p. 899.

49. "Day In, Day Out," *Nation and Athenaeum*, Aug. 11, 1928, p. 629.

50. "The Days of Dickens," *Nation and Athenaeum*, March 20, 1926, p. 870.

51. "Days That Are Gone," *Nation and Athenaeum*, July 5, 1924, p. 454.

52. "The Debtor," *TLS*, Nov. 17, 1905, p. 396.

53. "The Decay of Essay-Writing," *Academy and Literature*, Feb. 25, 1905, pp. 165-66.

54. "'Delta,'" *Guardian*, Dec. 13, 1905, p. 2131.

55. "A Description of the Desert," *Guardian*, Dec. 6, 1905, p. 2085.

56. "The Devil's Due," *Guardian*, Nov. 1, 1905, p. 1851.

57. "The Diaries of Mary, Countess of Meath," *Nation and Athenaeum*, Sept. 29, 1928, p. 832.

58. "Dickens by a Disciple," *TLS*, March 27, 1919, p. 163.

59. "A Disillusioned Romantic," *TLS*, July 1, 1920, p. 419.

60. "Dreams and Realities," *TLS*, May 30, 1918, p. 253.

61. "The Duke and Duchess of Newcastle-upon-Tyne," *TLS*, Feb. 2, 1911, p. 40.

62. "Editions-de-Luxe," *Nation and Athenaeum*, Aug. 23, 1924, pp. 645-46.

62a. "The English Mail Coach," *Guardian*, Oct. 3, 1906, pp. 1423-24.

63. "The Essays of Augustine Birrell," *Yale Review*(as "Augustine Birrell"), n.s. 19 (June 1930), 754-61; repr. w/var. in *Life and Letters*, 5 (July 1930), 29-38.

64. "Ethel Smyth," *New Statesman*, Apr. 23, 1921, pp. 80, 82.

65. "The Face of Clay," *TLS*, Apr. 13, 1906, p. 133.

66. "Fantasy," *TLS*, Dec. 15, 1921, p. 840.

67. "The Feminine Note in Fiction," *Guardian*, Jan. 25, 1905, p. 168.

68. CANCELLED

69. "'The Fighting Nineties,'" *TLS*, Oct. 12, 1916, p. 486.

70. "A Flood Tide," *TLS*, Nov. 17, 1905, p. 397.

71. "The Flurried Years," *Nation and Athenaeum*, March 20, 1926, pp. 870, 872.

72. "A Flying Lesson," *TLS*, Dec. 23, 1920, p. 873.

73. "Forgotten Benefactors," *Athenaeum*, July 4, 1919, pp. 555-56.

74. "The Fortunes of Farthings," *TLS*, March 31, 1905, p. 106.

75. "Frances Willard," *TLS*, Nov. 28, 1912, p. 544.

76. "Fraulein Schmidt and Mr. Anstruther," *TLS*, May 10, 1907, p. 149.

77. "From Hall-Boy to House-Steward," *Nation and Athenaeum*, Dec. 26, 1925, p. 476.

78. "Further Reminiscences, 1864-1894," *Nation and Athenaeum*, Apr. 18, 1925, p. 82.

79. "Gentlemen Errant," *TLS*, Apr. 15, 1909, p. 144.

80. "George Eliot," *Nation and Athenaeum*, Oct. 30, 1926, p. 149.

81. "Georgiana and Florence," *Listener*, Oct. 31, 1940, p. 639.

82. "Gipsy or Governess?" *Nation and Athenaeum*, May 16, 1925, p. 209.

83. "The Glen o'Weeping," *TLS*, May 24, 1907, p. 166.

84. "Glimpses of Authors," *Nation and Athenaeum*, Feb. 9, 1924, p. 678.

85. "A Good Daughter," *Daily Herald*, May 26, 1920, p. 7.

86. "Gorky on Tolstoi," *New Statesman*, Aug. 7, 1920, pp. 505-06.

87. "Great Men's Houses," *Good Housekeeping*, 21 (March 1932), 10-11, 102-03; repr. in Woolf, *The London Scene*. New York: Frank Hallman, [1975].

88. "Great Names: George Eliot," *Daily Herald*, March 9, 1921, p. 7.

89. "Guests and Memories," *Nation and Athenaeum*, Apr. 11, 1925, p. 54.

90. "Hearts of Controversy," *TLS*, Oct. 25, 1917, p. 515.

91. "Henley's Criticism," *TLS*, Feb. 24, 1921, p. 123.

92. "The Higher Court," *New Statesman*, Apr. 17, 1920, p. 44.

93. "The House of Lyme," *TLS*, March 29, 1917, p. 150.

94. "The House of Mirth," *Guardian*, Nov. 15, 1905, p. 1940.

95. "The House of Shadows," *TLS*, March 9, 1906, p. 84.

96. "How Should One Read a Book?" *Yale Review*, 16 (Oct. 1926, 32-44 [VERSION INDEXED HERE]; repr. (as "The Love of Reading") w/var. as Preface to *The Company of Books 1931-32*. The Hampshire Bookshop, 1932; repr. w/var. in Woolf, *Common Reader: Second Series*, 1932; repr. in *Scholastic* (New York), 33 (Nov. 12, 1938), 17E-18E, 24E; repr. in Woolf, *Collected Essays*, Vol. II, 1966. [Version indexed is from *Yale Review*]

97. "Imitative Essays," *TLS*, May 23, 1918, p. 243.

98. "The Immortal Isles," *Nation and Athenaeum*, March 5, 1927, pp. 766, 768.

99. "An Imperfect Lady," *TLS*, May 6, 1920, p. 283.

100. "An Impression of Gissing," *New Statesman*, June 30, 1923, pp. 371-72.

101. "In Good Company," *TLS*, Apr. 12, 1917, p. 175.

102. "In Memoriam: Caroline Emilia Stephen," *Guardian*, Apr. 21, 1909, pp. 636-37.

103. "In My Anecdotage," *Nation and Athenaeum*, Aug. 8, 1925, p. 576.

104. "Is This Poetry?" *Athenaeum*, June 20, 1919, p. 491.

105. "Jane Austen," *TLS*, May 8, 1913, pp. 189-90.

106. "Jane Austen at Sixty," *Nation and Athenaeum*, Dec. 15, 1923; repr. w/var. in *New Republic*, Jan. 30, 1924, p. 261.

107. "John Addington Symonds," *Nation and Athenaeum*, Apr. 18, 1925, p. 79; repr. in *New Republic*, June 3, 1925, pp. 51-52.

108. "John Davidson," *TLS*, Aug. 16, 1917, p. 390.

109. "Julia Margaret Cameron," Introduction to Cameron, *Victorian Photographs of Famous Men and Fair Women*. Hogarth Pr., 1926. Pp. 1-8.

110. "Lady Fanshawe's Memoirs," *TLS*, July 26, 1907, p. 234.

111. "Lady Ottoline Morrell," *The Times* (London), Apr. 28, 1938, p. 16.

112. "Lady Ritchie," *TLS*, March 6, 1919, p. 123.

113. "Landor in Little," *TLS*, Oct. 16, 1919, p. 564.

114. "The Last Days of Marie Antoinette," *TLS*, Nov. 7, 1907, p. 339.

115. "Laughter and Tears," *Nation and Athenaeum*, Oct. 16, 1926, p. 89.

116. "The Letter Killeth," *TLS*, Oct. 27, 1905, p. 359.

117. "Letters and Journals of Anne Chalmers," *Nation and Athenaeum*, Feb. 23, 1924, p. 746.

118. "Letters of Christina Rossetti," *TLS*, Nov. 12, 1908, p. 403.

119. "The Letters of Jane Welsh Carlyle," *Guardian*, Aug. 2, 1905, p. 1295.

120. "The Letters of Mary Russell Mitford," *Nation and Athenaeum*, Apr. 18, 1925, p. 82.

121. "The Life and Last Words of Wilfrid Ewart," *Nation and Athenaeum*, June 21, 1924, p. 392.

122. "The Limits of Perfection," *TLS*, Nov. 6, 1919, p. 627.

123. "London Revisited," *TLS*, Nov. 9, 1916, p. 535.

124. "Lone Marie," *Guardian*, Nov. 1, 1905, p. 1851.

125. "'Lord Jim,'" *TLS*, July 26, 1917, p. 355.

126. "Loud Laughter," *TLS*, June 20, 1918, p. 287.

127. "Louise de la Vallière," *Cornhill Magazine*, n.s. 25 (October 1908), 523-27.

128. "Madeleine," *TLS*, Oct. 9, 1919, p. 547.

129. "Mainly Victorian," *Nation and Athenaeum*, Apr. 11, 1925, p. 54.

130. "The Making of Michael," *TLS*, Nov. 17, 1905, p. 397.

131. "Marie Elizabeth Towneley: A Memoir," *Nation and Athenaeum*, June 7, 1924, p. 332.

132. "Mary Elizabeth Haldane," *Nation and Athenaeum*, Jan. 30, 1926, p. 624.

133. "Maturity and Immaturity," *Athenaeum*, Dec. 21, 1919, pp. 1220-21.

134. "Melba," *Nation and Athenaeum*, Dec. 5, 1925, p. 372.

135. "Melodious Meditations," *TLS*, Feb. 8, 1917, p. 67.

136. "The Memoirs of Lady Dorothy Nevill," *Cornhill Magazine*, n.s. 24 (April 1908), 469-73.

137. "Memories," *Nation and Athenaeum*, Nov. 17, 1928, p. 264.

138. "Memories and Notes," *Nation and Athenaeum*, Feb. 11, 1928, p. 728.

139. "Memories of a Militant," *Nation and Athenaeum*, Nov. 8, 1924, pp. 226, 228.

140. "Memories of Meredith," *TLS*, Dec. 18, 1919, p. 765.

141. "The Method of Henry James," *TLS*, Dec. 26, 1918, p. 655.

142. "The Mills of the Gods," *TLS*, June 17, 1920, p. 383.

143. "A Minor Dostoevsky," *TLS*, Oct. 11, 1917, p. 489.

144. "More Carlyle Letters," *TLS*, Apr. 1, 1909, p. 126.

145. "Mr. Bennett and Mrs. Brown," *Literary Review* of the
      New York Evening Post, 4 (Nov. 17, 1923), 153-54;
      repr. w/var. in *Nation and Athenaeum*, Dec. 1, 1923,
      pp. 342-43 [VERSION INDEXED HERE; KP C240; not to be
      confused with later versions of KP C251, which have
      the same name].

146. "Mr. Benson's Memories," *Nation and Athenaeum*, May
      10, 1924, p. 182.

147. "Mr. Conrad's Crisis," *TLS*, March 14, 1918, p. 126.

148. "Mr. Conrad's 'Youth,'" *TLS*, Sept. 20, 1917, p. 451.

149. "Mr. Gladstone's Daughter," *TLS*, Dec. 6, 1917, p.
      595.

150. "Mr. Gosse and His Friends," *TLS*, Oct. 2, 1919, p.
      529.

151. "Mr. Henry James's Latest Novel," *Guardian*, Feb. 22,
      1905, p. 339.

152. "Mr. Howells on Form," *TLS*, Nov. 14, 1918, p. 553.

153. "Mr. Symons's Essays," *TLS*, Dec. 21, 1916, p. 623.

154. "Mr. Yeats," *Nation and Athenaeum*, Apr. 21, 1928,
      p. 81.

155. "Mrs. Grundy's Crucifix," *TLS*, June 22, 1906, p. 226.

156. "Nancy Stair," *Guardian*, May 10, 1905, p. 803.

157. "'The New Crusade,'" *TLS*, Dec. 27, 1917, p. 647.

158. "The New Religion," *TLS*, Sept. 6, 1907, p. 269.

159. "Next-Door Neighbours," *Guardian*, Jan. 4, 1905, p.
      36.

160. "A Nineteenth-Century Critic," *Speaker*, Jan. 6, 1906,
      p. 352.

161. "The Novels of George Gissing," *TLS*, Jan. 11, 1912,
      pp. 9-10.

162. "Old and Young," *TLS*, Dec. 14, 1916, p. 608.

163. "An Old Novel," *TLS*, May 27, 1920, p. 333.

164. "On Not Knowing French," *New Republic*, Feb. 13, 1929,
      pp. 348-49.

165. "On Some of the Old Actors," *Athenaeum*, June 6, 1919,
      pp. 427-28.

166. "On the Stage," *Nation and Athenaeum*, June 30, 1928, p. 436.

167. "Paradise in Piccadilly," *Nation and Athenaeum*, March 6, 1926, p. 786.

168. "Parodies," *TLS*, March 8, 1917, p. 112.

169. "Past and Present at the English Lakes," *TLS*, June 29, 1916, p. 307.

170. "'Pattledom,'" *Nation and Athenaeum*, Aug. 1, 1925, p. 427.

171. "Peggy," *Nation and Athenaeum*, Nov. 8, 1924, p. 228.

172. "The Perfect Language," *TLS*, May 24, 1917, p. 247.

173. "Philip Sidney," *TLS*, May 31, 1907, pp. 173-74.

174. "Pictures and Portraits," *Athenaeum*, Jan. 9, 1920, pp. 46-47.

175. "A Player Under Three Reigns," *Nation and Athenaeum*, Apr. 25, 1925, p. 114.

176. "Plays ... ," *Nation and Athenaeum*, Nov. 17, 1928, p. 255.

177. "The Poems ... of ... Lord Herbert of Cherbury," *Nation and Athenaeum*, Jan. 19, 1924, p. 584.

178. "The Poetic Drama," *Guardian*, Apr. 18, 1906, p. 651.

179. "Poets' Letters," *Speaker*, Apr. 21, 1906, pp. 63-64.

180. "Portraits of Places," *Guardian*, Oct. 3, 1906, p. 1631.

181. "A Positivist," *TLS*, July 17, 1919, p. 386.

182. "A Practical Utopia," *TLS*, Aug. 15, 1918, p. 380.

183. "Preferences ... ," *New York Herald Tribune Books*, Apr. 15, 1928, p. 1.

184. "A Prince of Prose," *TLS*, March 3, 1921, p. 141.

185. "'The Private Papers of Henry Ryecroft,'" *Guardian*, Feb. 13, 1907, pp. 282-83.

186. "Pure English," *TLS*, July 15, 1920, p. 453.

187. "Queen Alexandra the Well-Beloved," *Nation and Athenaeum*, Feb. 6, 1926, p. 654.

188. "Rachel," *TLS*, Apr. 20, 1911, p. 155.

189.   "The Reader," *Twentieth Century Literature*, 25
        (Fall/Winter 1979), 427-35.

190.   "Real Letters," *TLS*, Nov. 6, 1919, p. 627.

191.   "Rebels and Reformers," *TLS*, Dec. 20, 1917, p. 634.

192.   "Recent Paintings of Vanessa Bell," Foreword to Lon-
        don Artists' Association Catalogue, 1930. Pp. [2-5].

192a.   " ... Recent Paintings of Vanessa Bell," Foreword to
        Lefevre Galleries Catalogue, 1934. P. [1].

193.   "Reminiscences of Mrs. Comys Carr," *Nation and Ath-
        enaeum*, March 20, 1926, p. 870.

194.   "Restoration Comedy," *Nation and Athenaeum*, Oct. 18,
        1924, p. 122; repr. in *New Republic*, Feb. 11, 1925,
        pp. 315-16.

195.   "Richard Hakluyt," *Nation and Athenaeum*, Oct. 25,
        1924, p. 164.

196.   "Robert Smith Surtees," *Nation and Athenaeum*, June
        21, 1924, p. 392.

197.   "Romance," *TLS*, Jan. 18, 1917, p. 31.

198.   "Romance and the 'Nineties," *Nation and Athenaeum*,
        July 3, 1926, p. 392.

199.   "Rose of Lone Farm," *Guardian*, July 19, 1905, p.
        1224.

200.   "The Russian View," *TLS*, Dec. 19, 1918, p. 641.

201.   "The Sad Years," *TLS*, Aug. 29, 1918, p. 403.

202.   "Saint Samuel of Fleet Street," *Nation and Athenaeum*,
        Nov. 14, 1925, p. 248; repr. w/var. in *New Republic*,
        Jan. 6, 1926, p. 197.

203.   "The Scholar's Daughter," *TLS*, Feb. 16, 1906, p. 52.

204.   "The Schoolroom Floor," *TLS*, Oct. 2, 1924, p. 609.

205.   "Scottish Women," *TLS*, Sept. 3, 1908, p. 284.

206.   "Scott's Character," *TLS*, Apr. 28, 1921, p. 273.

207.   "Second Marriage," *TLS*, Apr. 25, 1918, p. 195.

208.   "Sir Thomas Browne," *TLS*, June 28, 1923, p. 436.

209.   "The Sister of Frederic the Great," *Academy*, 13
        (January 1906), 35-36.

210. "Small Talk About Meredith," *TLS*, Feb. 13, 1919, p. 81.

211. "Smoke Rings and Roundelays," *Nation and Athenaeum*, Oct. 25, 1924, p. 164.

212. "Social Life in England," *TLS*, Dec. 21, 1916, p. 620.

213. "Some of the Smaller Manor Houses of Sussex," *Nation and Athenaeum*, Dec. 5, 1925, p. 382.

214. "Somehow Good," *TLS*, Feb. 6, 1908, p. 45.

215. "The Son of Royal Langbrith," *Guardian*, Dec. 14, 1904, p. 2120.

216. "Stalky's Reminiscences," *Nation and Athenaeum*, Apr. 7, 1928, p. 22.

217. "Steeple-Jacks and Steeplejacking," *Nation and Athenaeum*, March 27, 1926, p. 906.

218. "Stendhal," *Nation and Athenaeum*, July 5, 1924, p. 452.

219. "Stendhal," *Adam International Review*, Thirty-seventh Year (1972), 364-66.

220. "Stopford Brooke," *TLS*, Nov. 29, 1917, p. 581.

221. "The Stranger in London," *TLS*, July 30, 1908, p. 244.

222. "The Sunset," in Frederic William Maitland, *The Life and Letters of Leslie Stephen*. Duckworth, 1906. Pp. 474-76.

223. "Sunset Reflections," *TLS*, Dec. 20, 1917, p. 636.

224. "A Supreme Moment," *TLS*, Feb. 16, 1906, p. 52.

225. "A Swan and Her Friends," *TLS*, Nov. 14, 1907, p. 348.

226. "Sweetness--Long Drawn Out," *Academy*, July 28, 1906, p. 81.

227. "Swinburne Letters," *TLS*, March 21, 1918, p. 139.

228. "The Tale of Genji," *Vogue*, 66 (late July 1925), 53, 80.

229. "A Talker," *TLS*, Apr. 12, 1917, p. 173.

230. "Tchehov's Questions," *TLS*, May 16, 1918, p. 231.

231. "Temptation," *TLS*, Feb. 22, 1907, p. 62.

232. "Their Passing Hour," *Academy*, Aug. 26, 1905, pp. 871-72.

233. "These Were Muses," *Nation and Athenaeum*, Nov. 22, 1924, p. 297.

234. "This for Remembrance," *Nation and Athenaeum*, March 28, 1925, p. 896.

235. "Three Characters," *Adam International Review*, Thirty-seventh Year (1972), 364-66.

236. "Time, Taste,and Furniture," *Nation and Athenaeum*, Aug. 15, 1925, p. 604.

237. "Tolstoy's 'The Cossacks,'" *TLS*, Feb. 1, 1917, p. 55.

238. "To Read or Not to Read," *TLS*, Sept. 6, 1917, p. 427.

239. "The Tower of Siloam," *Guardian*, Dec. 20, 1905, p. 1272.

240. "Trafficks and Discoveries," *Speaker*, Aug. 11, 1906, pp. 440-41.

241. "Trafficks and Discoveries," *TLS*, Dec. 12, 1918, p. 618.

242. "The Tragic Life of Vincent Van Gogh," *Nation and Athenaeum*, May 9, 1925, p. 182.

243. "Trousers," *New Statesman*, June 4, 1921, pp. 252, 254.

244. "The Truth at Last," *Nation and Athenaeum*, July 19, 1924, p. 518.

245. "Twenty Years of My Life," *Nation and Athenaeum*, Oct. 17, 1925, p. 126.

246. "Two Irish Novels," *TLS*, Dec. 15, 1905, p. 445.

247. "Two Irish Poets," *TLS*, May 2, 1918, p. 206.

248. "The Two Samuel Butlers," *Nation and Athenaeum*, Apr. 11, 1925, pp. 53-54.

249. "Unknown Essex," *Nation and Athenaeum*, Aug. 8, 1925, pp. 575-76.

250. "Unpublished Letters of Matthew Arnold," *Nation and Athenaeum*, Feb. 16, 1924, p. 712.

251. "Unwritten History," *Nation and Athenaeum*, June 21, 1924, p. 392.

252. "Valery Brussof," *TLS*, Oct. 24, 1918, p. 509.

253. "A Vanished Generation," *TLS*, Dec. 3, 1908, p. 445.

254. "Venice," *TLS*, Jan. 7, 1909, pp. 5-6.

255. "A Victorian Echo," *TLS*, Aug. 23, 1917, p. 403.

256. "Victorian Jottings," *Nation and Athenaeum*, Feb. 12, 1927, p. 672.

257. "A Victorian Socialist," *TLS*, June 27, 1918, p. 299.

258. "A View of the Russian Revolution," *TLS*, Dec. 19, 1918, p. 636.

259. "The War from the Street," *TLS*, Jan. 9, 1919, p. 14.

260. "Washington Irving," *TLS*, Apr. 3, 1919, p. 179.

261. "Watts-Dunton's Dilemma," *TLS*, Dec. 11, 1919, p. 730.

262. "The Week End," *TLS*, July 3, 1924, p. 416.

263. "A Week in the White House," *Cornhill Magazine*, n.s. 25 (August 1908), 217-22.

264. "What Is a Novel?" *Weekly Dispatch*, March 27, 1927, p. 2; repr. in *Now and Then*, Summer 1927, p. 16.

265. "William Allingham," *TLS*, Dec. 19, 1907, p. 387.

266. "Wordsworth and the Lakes," *TLS*, June 15, 1906, p. 216.

267. "Wordsworth Letters," *TLS*, Apr. 2, 1908, pp. 108-09.

268. "The Wrong Way of Reading," *Athenaeum*, May 18, 1920, pp. 695-97.

SECOND ADDENDUM TO *CATALOGUE OF BOOKS*
FROM THE LIBRARY OF LEONARD AND VIRGINIA WOOLF
TAKEN FROM MONKS HOUSE, RODMELL, SUSSEX AND 24
VICTORIA SQUARE, LONDON AND NOW IN THE POSSESSION OF
WASHINGTON STATE UNIVERSITY, PULLMAN, U.S.A.
(Brighton: Holleyman and Treacher, 1975)

I. Books Belonging to the Woolfs, Acquired from Quentin
   and Anne Olivier Bell, Spring 1983, by Washington
   State University

Arnold, Matthew. *Culture and Anarchy, an Essay.* Popular
   ed. Smith, Elder, 1901.

Arnold, Matthew. *Essays in Criticism. Second Series.*
   Macmillan, 1906.

Arnold, Matthew. *The Study of Celtic Literature.* Popular
   ed. Smith, Elder, 1891. Belonged to Virginia.

Bacon, Francis. *The Letters and the Life of ... , Includ-*
   ing All His Occasional Works Namely Letters ... with
   a Commentary Biographical ..., ed. by James
   Spedding. 7 vol. Longman, Green, Longman and Roberts, 1861-74. Vols. I-II (1861-62) only. [Vols.
   III-VII are listed in Holleyman.]

Balzac, Honoré de. *Oeuvres Complètes.* Nouvelle ed. Paris: M. Levy Frères, 1856. 45 vol. Vol. X missing.

Byron, George Gordon Noel, Lord. (See under Moore, Thomas.)

Carlyle, Jane Welsh. *Early Letters of Jane Welsh Car-*
   lyle, Together with a Few of Later Years ... All
   Hitherto Unpublished ... , ed. by David G.M.A. Ritchie. Swan Sonnenschein, 1889.

Carlyle, Jane Welsh. *Letters and Memorials of Jane Welsh*
   Carlyle. Prepared for Publication by Thomas Carlyle,
   ed. by James Anthony Froude. 3 vol. Longmans,
   Green, 1883. Belonged to Leslie Stephen.

Carlyle, Thomas. *The Collected Works of....* 16 vol. Chapman and Hall, 1857-58. [Vols. IV and XIV are listed
   in Holleyman.] Belonged to Leslie Stephen. Vol. XIII
   missing.

Carlyle, Thomas. *The French Revolution, a History.* 3
    vol. Chapman and Hall, 1898. Belonged to Thoby Ste-
    phen.

Carlyle, Thomas. *Reminiscences,* ed. by James Anthony
    Froude. 2 vol. Longmans, Green, 1881.

Clemens, Samuel Langhorne [Mark Twain]. *Life on the Mis-
    sissippi.* Chatto and Windus, 1883.

Cobbett, William. *Rural Rides in the Counties ... with
    Economical ... Observations.* A. Cobbett, 1853. Be-
    longed to Leslie Stephen.

Eliot, George. *The Popular Short Tales of ... , with a
    Biographical Sketch.* Simpkin, Marshall, Hamilton,
    Kent; Glasgow: Thomas D. Morrison, n.d.[?]. Be-
    longed to Virginia.

FitzGerald, Edward. *Dictionary of Madame de Sévigné,* ed.
    and annotated by Mary Eleanor Fitzgerald Kerrich. 2
    vol. Macmillan, 1914.

Fox, Caroline. *Memories of Old Friends, Being Extracts
    from the Journals of,* ed. by Horace N. Pym. 3rd ed.
    2 vol. Smith, Elder, 1882. Belonged to Virginia.

Hakluyt, Richard. *Hakluyt's Collection of the Early Voy-
    ages, Travels, and Discoveries of the English Nation.*
    New ed., with additions. 5 vol. R.H. Evans, J. Mac-
    kinley and R. Priestly, 1808. Belonged to Virginia.

Hume, David. *Four Dissertations: 1) The Natural History
    of Religion, 2) Of the Passions, 3) Of Tragedy, 4) Of
    the Standard of Taste.* A. Millar, 1757. Belonged to
    Leslie Stephen.

James, William. *The Will to Believe and Other Essays in
    Popular Philosophy.* Longmans, Green, 1897. Belonged
    to Leslie Stephen.

[Johnstone, Charles]. *Chrysal: Or the Adventures of a Gui-
    nea.* 4 vol. Vols. I (7th ed., 1771), III (2nd ed.,
    1767), and IV (2nd ed., 1767) only. N.p.

Lee, Sir Sidney, editor. *Dictionary of National Biography.*
    22 vol. Oxford U. Pr., 1896. Belonged to Leslie Ste-
    phen (co-editor).

Lowell, James Russell. *Among My Books. Second Series.*
    Boston: James R. Osgood, 1876. Belonged to Leslie
    Stephen.

Lowell, James Russell. *Letters of*, ed. by Charles Eliot Norton. 2 vol. Osgood, McIlvaine, 1894. Duplicate of edition already received (see Holleyman), but belonged to Gerald Duckworth.

Lowell, James Russell. *The Writings of*.... Riverside ed. 10 vol. Macmillan, 1890. Vol. IX (*Poems* ...) only.

Mill, John Stuart. *Autobiography*. Longmans, Green, Reader and Dyer, 1873. Belonged to Leslie Stephen.

Mill, John Stuart. *On Liberty*. John W. Parker, 1859. Belonged to Leslie Stephen.

Moore, Thomas. *The Life, Letters and Journals of Lord Byron*, ed. by Sir Walter Scott. New ed. Murray, 1866. Belonged to Leslie Stephen.

Morley, John. *On Compromise*. Chapman and Hall, 1874.

Percy, Thomas. *Reliques of Ancient English Poetry* ..., ed. by J.V. Prichard. 2 vol. G. Bell, 1876. Belonged to Stella Duckworth.

Procter, Adelaide Anne. *Legends and Lyrics, a Book of Verses*. 2nd ed. Bell and Daldy, 1858.

Renan, Ernest. *Vie de Jesus*. 3rd ed. Paris: Michel Levy Frères, 1867. Belonged to Leslie Stephen.

Ritchie, Anne Isabella (Thackeray). *A Book of Sibyls: Mrs. Barbauld, Mrs. Opie, Miss Edgeworth, Miss Austen*. Smith, Elder, 1883. Belonged to Julia Stephen.

Ritchie, Anne Isabella (Thackeray). *Mrs. Dymond*. Smith, Elder, 1885. Belonged to Leslie Stephen.

Ritchie, Anne Isabella (Thackeray). *To Esther and Other Sketches*. Smith, Elder, 1869. Belonged to Laura Makepeace Stephen.

Spenser, Edmund. *The Works of*, ed. by J. Payne Collier. 5 vol. Bell and Daldy, 1862. Belonged to L. Stephen.

Stephen, H[arry] L[ushington], editor. *State Trials, Political and Social*. 2 vol. Duckworth, 1899. Vol. I only.

Stephen, James. *Considerations on Imprisonment for Debt*. ... T. Evans, 1770. Belonged to Leslie Stephen.

Stephen, Sir James. *Lectures on the History of France*. 2nd ed. 2 vol. Longman, Brown, Green and Longmans; Cambridge: J. Deighton and Macmillan, 1852.

Stephen, Leslie. *An Agnostic's Apology and Other Essays*. Smith, Elder, 1893.

Stephen, Leslie. *English Literature and Society in the Eighteenth Century*. Duckworth, 1904.

Stephen, Leslie. *The English Utilitarians*. 3 vol. Duckworth, 1900. Belonged to Virginia.

Stephen, Leslie. *The English Utilitarians*. Library ed. 3 vol. Duckworth, [1912].

Stephen, Leslie. *History of English Thought in the Eighteenth Century*. 2 vol. Smith, Elder, 1876. Belonged to Julia Stephen.

Stephen, Leslie. *Hours in a Library*. New ed., with additions. 3 vol. Smith, Elder, 1892. Belonged to Virginia.

Stephen, Leslie. *The Life of Sir James Fitzjames Stephen, Bart*. Smith, Elder, 1895. Belonged to Thoby Stephen.

Stephen, Leslie. *The Playground of Europe*. Longmans, Green, 1901.

Stephen, Leslie. *The Science of Ethics*. Smith, Elder, 1882.

Stephen, Leslie. *Sketches from Cambridge*. Macmillan, 1865.

Stephen, Leslie. *Social Rights and Duties: Addresses to Ethical Societies*. 2 vol. Swan Sonnenschein; New York: Macmillan, 1896. Vol. II only.

Stephen, Leslie. *Studies of a Biographer*. 2 vol. Duckworth, 1898.

Stephen, Leslie. *Studies of a Biographer. Second Series*. 2 vol. Duckworth, 1902.

Stephen, Leslie. *The "Times" on the American War, a Historical Study*. William Ridgway, 1865. [Cf. Holleyman Addendum.]

Stephen, Leslie. *The Writings of W.M. Thackeray*. N.p.: n.d. "Pp. 305-367." [Torn out of Vol. XXIV of *Works of W.M. Thackeray*. 26 vol. DeLuxe Ed. Smith, Elder, 1878-86.]

Stevenson, Robert Louis. *An Inland Voyage*. Chatto and Windus, 1900.

Thackeray, William Makepeace. *The History of Pendennis.
His Fortunes....* 2 vol. Bradbury and Evans, 1849-50.

Thackeray, William Makepeace. *Miscellanies: Prose and
Verse.* 4 vol. Bradbury, Evans, 1855 -57. Belonged
to Leslie Stephen. Includes 2 copies of Vol. IV.

Thackeray, William Makepeace. *The Newcomes, Memoirs of a
Most Respectable Family.* 2 vol. Bradbury and Evans,
1854-55.

Thackeray, William Makepeace. *Thackerayana, Notes and
Anecdotes.* Chatto and Windus, 1875. Belonged to L.S.

Thackeray, William Makepeace. *Vanity Fair; a Novel Without
a Hero.* Bradbury and Evans, 1849.

Thackeray, William Makepeace. *The Virginians, a Tale of
the Last Century* . 2 vol. Bradbury and Evans, 1858-
59. Belonged to Leslie Stephen.

Walpole, Horace. *The Letters of,* ed. by Peter Cunningham.
9 vol. R. Bentley, 1858. Vol. VII only. [Vols. I-
VI, VIII-IX are listed in Holleyman.]

II. Ambiguous Items as Listed by Holleyman: Supplement
to List in *Virginia Woolf's Literary Sources and Allusions: A Guide to the Essays*

INCOMPLETE LISTINGS

"Come Hither. Collection of Rhymes &c." 1928. (Index,
p. 14; "Monks House Catalogue," Sec. 5, p. 17)
De la Mare, Walter, comp. *Come Hither.* Constable, 1928.
[According to Holleyman system, should be under "Various
Authors."]

"The History of Nourjahad." 1927. (Index, p. 58; "Monks
House Catalogue," Sec. 5, p. 14)
[Sheridan, Frances]. *The History of Nourjahad by the
Editor of Sidney Bidulph.* London: Elkin Mathews and Mar-
rot, 1927. (Orig. 1767; F. Sheridan's dates were 1724-66)

LISTED UNDER "ANON." (Index, p. 2)

"Arbiter in Council." 1906.
Hirst, Francis Wrigley. *The Arbiter in Council.* Macmillan, 1906. ["Victoria Square Catalogue," Sec. 5, p. 11]

"Bubbles by an Old Man." 1837.
[Head, Sir Francis]. *Bubbles by an Old Man.* Paris: Casimir, 1837. ["Victoria Square Catalogue," Sec. 1, p. 36]
This belonged to Leslie Stephen.

"Considerations sur les Cauces [sic] de la Grandeur des Romains et de leur Décadence." 1755.
[Montesquieu, Charles Louis de Secondat]. *Considerations sur les Causes de la Grandeur des Romains, et de leur Décadence.* New ed. Paris: Chez Guillyn, 1755. ["Victoria Square Catalogue," Sec. 1, p. 33] This belonged to Leslie Stephen.

"Euphrosyne." 1905.
[Bell, Clive, Lytton Strachey, Leonard Woolf, *et al.*]
Euphrosyne. A Collection of Verse. Cambridge: E. Johnson, 1905. ["Victoria Square Catalogue," Sec. 5, p. 73] (See Quentin Bell, *Virginia Woolf.* New York: Harcourt Brace Jovanovich, 1972. Vol. I, pp. 98, 205-06.) [According to Holleyman system, should be under "Various Authors."]

*LISTED UNDER "VARIOUS AUTHORS"** (Index, pp. 61-62)
[* "Various" = "several in one work"]

"Chief Pre-Shakespearean Dramas." 1925.
Adams, Joseph Quincy, ed. *Chief Pre-Shakespearean Dramas.* G.G. Harrap, [1925]. ["Victoria Square Catalogue," Sec. 5, p. 48]

"Modern English Essays 1870-1920." 1922.
R[hys], E[rnest], ed. *Modern English Essays. 1870-1920.* 5 vol. J.M. Dent, 1922. ["Victoria Square Catalogue," Sec. 5, p. 77]
Woolf reviewed this for *TLS*, Nov. 30, 1922, pp. 769-70; see "The Modern Essay," *Common Reader I.*

III. Pamphlets (not Books) on Authors and Writing, Sold to Washington State University by Holleyman, but Omitted from Catalogue

Bridges, J.H. *The Unity of Comte's Life and Doctrine.* N. Trübner, 1866.

Clynes, J.R. *When I Remember.* Macmillan War Pamphlets #6. Macmillan, 1940.

The Craft of Printing. Supplement to the *Manchester Guardian*, May 23, 1922.

Forster, E[dward] M[organ]. *Nordic Twilight.* Macmillan War Pamphlets #3. Macmillan, 1940.

George Sand. Paris: Albert Morancé, n.d.

Gordan, George. *Shakespeare's English*. S.P.E. Tract #29. Oxford: Clarendon, 1928.

Hartog, Sir Philip[pe] Joseph. *On the Relation of Poetry to Verse*. English Association Pamphlet #64. Oxford: Univ. Pr., 1926.

The Hogarth Press. Catalogues of ... beginning with *The Complete Catalogue of the Hogarth Press, 1917-1927*. [A run of catalogues, flyers and leaflets describing books published by the Woolfs]

Maude, Aylmer. *Tolstoy on Art and Its Critics*. Oxford Univ. Pr., 1925.

Roberts, S[ydney] C[astle]. *Lord Macaulay*. English Association Pamphlet #67. Oxford: Univ. Pr., 1927.

Scott, Fred Newton. *American Slang*. S.P.E. Tract #24. [Oxford:] Clarendon, 1926.

INDEX

INDEX OF AUTHORS AND WORKS
NAMED IN THE REDISCOVERED ESSAYS
AND IN THE CHARTS, CHAPTER 4, ABOVE

(Arabic numerals indicate the assigned numbers of the rediscovered essays [see Appendix A, pp. 203-15]; italicized
numbers refer to pages of the appropriate charts [pp. 42-
199].)